Thy Kingdom Come

"Living A Life With Dominion, Power and Authority"

Authors
Minister Andrea D. Wilson
Minister Tamora R. Walls
Minister Eunice Wade

Foreword
Rev. Jacquie Hood-Martin

The Word Publishing, LLC.

The Word Publishing, LLC.
wordpublishing@wordkingdom.org

Requests for information should be mailed to:
The Word Publishing, LLC.
P.O. Box 68094
Shaumburg, IL 60168

The Word Publishing books may be purchased for educational, business, or sales promotional use. For information please write:

Special Markets Department
P.O. Box 68094
Shaumburg, IL 60168
wordpublishing@wordkingdom.org

Published by The Word Publishing, LLC.
ISBN: 978-0-9816871-0-0

Cover design and inside pages by Tamora R. Walls

Kudos for "Thy Kingdom Come"

"What does having a meaningful and fruitful life mean to you? How do you attain the desires of your heart for living a purposeful life?

There are many questions that we want answered. Well, many answers can be found in this wonderful work.

This book examines and answers questions relating to God's will and His promises for Kingdom living on this earth. In this writing, we learn, very clearly, how to incorporate God's will for us in our everyday living. We learn that the path for attaining the fulfillment and responsibility that God has intended for us exists within us. All we need to do is to listen to the soft voice of God that dwells within us and follow the mandates proscribed in His word.

This book is refreshing and well written. The scenarios allow one to apply their personal circumstances and find answers to satisfy personal needs.

On the pages that follow, begin your journey and do not stop until the very last page!"

Honorable Donna Phelps Felton

◇◇

"I have several books that I keep beside by bed. These books include the most celebrated business books on various topics and also the Holy Bible. When I was given a copy of this book it soon became a bedside favorite. As a successful businessman I have finally found a book that can help me be a better Christian, husband, father and business man.

These ladies have done it! If you want to know how to live a prosperous life in every area, this is the book for you. I recommend this book at the top of my list for success. You can have it all and this book proves it. Thank you ministers, for being obedient to the call of God."

D. Dominick Davidson, Consultant

◇◇

"I am what most would call a 'babe in Christ'. I have searched to strengthen my relationship with God and this book gave me a clearer understanding of my purpose in life and also the awesome love Christ has for me. This book gave me the tools needed to obtain the life Christ died to give me. Thank you to the Ambassadors for writing a book for this generation of believers."

Michael Grant, Entrepreneur

DEDICATIONS

To the great congregation of Word Kingdom Ministries, your love, support, loyalty and enthusiasm are second to none. We are committed and dedicated to you. We are committed to helping you live a life as God's Ambassadors. We are dedicated to changing the world. Our latter shall be greater!

And to every Kingdom Believer, may this book propel you into the best days of your life.

Love,
The Ambassadors

Thy Kingdom Come
TABLE OF CONTENTS

Foreword: Rev. Jacquie Martin Hood

"Behold I stand at the door and knock"
(Revelation 3:1-22)
Mending America's Broken Soul
Rev. Jacquie Martin Hood

Growing up in communities across the country, people would use an old adage 'if it ain't broke don't fix it!' Over time what this has come to mean is that the problem is too big for me as one person to solve, so I why bother trying. This apathetic approach to life and dealing with life's problem has become a resounding sentiment in the country we call America.

People in history, Gandhi, Mother Theresa, Elijah Muhammad, the Kennedy's, Malcolm X, Martin Luther King, Jr., Minister Louis Farrakhan, Rev. Al Sharpton, Rev. Jesse Jackson, Roland S. Martin, Tavis Smiley, elected officials, political pundits, blue collar comedians, and ordinary people like you and me, have become fixated on solving the ills of American society. It seems that we spend at a lot time talking at each, rather than to each other. What we can do, is begin the dialogue about where we are, where we want to go, and how do we get there for the good of the nation. It is not beyond our ability. The world in which we live is not perfect. It never has been and probably never will be. The phrases in the Lord's Prayer "thy kingdom come, thy will be done, on earth as it is in heaven", gives us a glimpse of what could be, if we put our all in all in Him. The questions I raise are "Does America desire to be healed?" "Do you want to be healed?"

THY KINGDOM COME

In the midst of danger, in the face of adversity, in the presence of strife, or in the throws of overcoming insurmountable odds, men and women of God have risen to the occasion of finding a way to move past their problems and sought to fix their own broken soul.

"Getting on a path for life is easy. Learning to stay on that path is where the work begins. All through our lives, we begin on a course of one direction or another. Our parents set the pace for us and we navigate the best we know how once we are on our own. Yet, without continual guidance, our path clutters quickly and we can lose our way. It is with this sense of longing to get on point and stay on point that we must look at how we got to where we are; realizing the same course of action or inaction cannot take us where we desire to go". *(Reclaiming Your Life, ROMAR 2007)*

It is through our individual healing that a collective healing ensues.

The fever pitch of the 2008 Presidential election sent America into a tailspin. The eyes of the world are opening to the hurt and pain suffered by many through generations of decision-making that has a stranglehold on its people. The opening of this proverbial Pandora's Box is causing self-reflection and introspection, having us question our motives, second guessing our actions, and wondering if we have been living a lie, built on others greed and deception. What we have discovered is that some issues we face are bigger than we are. Decisions bigger than us require a solution that has nothing to do directly with us, yet is one that requires us to participate fully, and without reservation. I am not a cynic. I am the ultimate optimist, a true believer in the Word of God, and a person who is experiencing the abundant blessings of God just as He promised in His Word I would receive. My doubt is in people who profess to be believers, yet are unwilling to give themselves fully over to Gods' use for work in the Kingdom of God. The scripture says, "The harvest is plentiful, but the laborers are few" (Luke 10:2). The journey for all of us begins one person at a time; and, for every person who receives a healing, they move on to help others through the healing process.

Today, I challenge you to walk toward the will of God and embrace the work in which He has you to do. If you are ready, when you are ready, take a leap of faith and listen to a message on my website www.jacquiehood.com entitled "No Fear". It is true, that "God hath not given us the spirit of fear; but of power, and of love, and of a sound mind" *(2 Timothy 1:7)*.

The Spirit of the Lord will touch your heart as you ease into doing the work God has prepared for you to do. There is no greater joy in life!

Jacquie Hood-Martin
www.jacquiehood.com

If you are ready to live life as an Ambassador on the earth…if you want to live the best life possible… now is the time.

Thy Kingdom Come on earth begins with you turning the page!

Why Ambassador?

Throughout this book you will see that we refer to ourselves as "Ambassadors" and you may wonder why. The dictionary defines ambassador this way:

A diplomatic official of the highest rank appointed. A representative appointed and accredited in residence by one government or sovereign to another, usually for a specific amount of time. An ambassador carries out his/her country's permanent mission while residing in another country. An ambassador is an authorized messenger or representative.

When Jesus prays for his disciples in John chapter 17 he says this to His father:

I have given them your word and the world has hated them, for they are not of the world any more than I am of the world. My prayer is not that you take them out of the world but that you protect them from the evil one. They are not of the world, even as I am not of it. Sanctify them by the truth; your word is truth. As you sent me into the world, I have sent them into the world. For them I sanctify myself, that they too may be truly sanctified.
(John 17:14-19 ~ NIV)

Jesus, an Ambassador from heaven was sent to the earth with a purpose. When you were born, you were born also with a divine purpose. In this passage of scripture we can clearly see we are ambassadors appointed by the highest official of heaven. We are here for a specific amount of time. We are representatives, authorized messengers for Jesus Christ. We are all Ambassadors.

God, Man, and the Kingdom
Ambassador Walls

Have you ever looked inside of a mechanical object just to see how it works and upon opening it you enter into a place of both unfamiliar and familiar objects? Take a watch for example. When you look inside a watch there are many parts, some big and some small, all working together for the total purpose of giving the illustration of time moving forward. Notice I said the illustration of time moving forward and not the actual watch itself moving time forward. For without the watch time would continue to move even though visually you would not see it; which is why when you don't have a watch you may ask someone, "What time is it?"

The inside parts of a watch all work together systematically to create the real illustration of time. Our lives work the same way and even this book was cultivated for the sole purpose to have us look at the inner parts of the Kingdom and see what those parts are and how they work together in order to see the illustration of how Kingdom living should look. We must understand before going any further, just like the watch we know that time exists even if we don't have a watch. So it is the same with the Kingdom in heaven and on earth exist even if we're not living it. So, let's discover what God created and see how it all works together.

The Beginning

In order to examine anything in life and receive clear understanding you must start with the beginning, and the creator. For us this would mean examining the writings which give us the illustration of the Kingdom; which is the "bible". The first book of the bible, which is Genesis, begins with these words; "In the beginning". Here we see that in the beginning God creates from a voided earth a world that would later belong to man and it would be his "heavenly Kingdom on earth". We also discover how the kingdom on earth functioned and how man operated in authority as an "Ambassador". In Genesis 1: 26 God said, *"Let us make man in our image, in our likeness, and let them rule over the fish of the sea and the birds of the air, over the livestock, over all the earth, and over all the creatures that move along the ground."*

Since we were created in God's image this ultimately means we embody the qualities and characteristics of God, the Son, and the Holy Spirit. All of mankind has these three but not all mankind operate in them or even give acknowledgement that they dwell down on the inside. Inside each of us lies all of the intricate parts to help us live a Kingdom life because we were made in His image: with authority (God), a visual body (Son), and power (Holy Spirit); all working together to perform a glorious work for the Kingdom.

The Purpose for Our Existence

Have you ever thought to yourself why did God go through all of this to create us and create a place for us to live? I would suggest he did it because God is "Love" and love always shares its very best. Since God is love that would surely mean God had to share Himself. In fact love can not operate in any other way. It must share of itself. 1 John 4:16 says *"And so we know and rely on the love God has for us. God is love. Whoever lives in love lives in God, and God in him."*

THY KINGDOM COME

God is in us when we live in love and it is a part of our makeup. When we operate in love we are a part of God. That is why Romans 8:39 tell us that nothing can separate us from the love of God because we are intertwined with Him through His love. It is this same love that God has for us that we should give to others. God gave us Jesus, His only begotten Son, who showed us what love is supposed to look like and it is this same love that will draw us out of the earth and into kingdom living. The earth system would have you to believe that you must sell, bargain, negotiate, outwit or even lose yourself in order to have control and feel loved. This is what we call "conditional" love. Conditional love is controlling and possessive. This kind of love embodies the insecurities of the person exercising it. The voice of conditional love would say:

"I want you to love me this way.
"I did this for you so you owe me this".
"It's going to go my way no matter what you say".

Conditional love feeds an insecurity of one of the persons by attaching conditions and rules. Having these kinds of relationships is damaging and will eventually kill the spirit of both persons. Don't we see these people everyday that are trapped and have suppressed their feelings because they think that love operates this way? This is why God teaches us to have "unconditional love", where there are no strings attached. This love is not looking to get anything back in return as payback but it looks to see that the fulfillment of the mission is accomplished and brings joy in the place of sorrow, hope in the place of hopelessness, and fullness in the place of void. Love gives and does not take. Love deposits and does not extract from. It was God that give a part of Himself for mankind and not only did He give himself, but gave man a replica of Heaven and made a heaven on earth for him to dwell in. Here in Genesis God created everything that man would need in this place called "paradise" or the "Garden of Eden". This is the place that man would call home and it would be man's responsibility to rule and have dominion.

Partnerships in the Earth

We also see the development of the first partnerships between God and Man and Man and Woman. In Genesis 1:26 God says, let us make man. Then he commands let *"them"* have dominion. Note here that He did not say and let "us and man" have dominion. It is here at the very beginning we see God establish partnership. Through this divine partnership God appoints His authority to man to have dominion over everything that He created on the earth. The definition of dominion is to have control or the exercise of control over a territory and have "influence". In essence, man became the next responsible person in line. There was no other living thing on earth that had authority and power except man who was appointed by God. God gave Adam (the first man) responsibility to then name every living thing that God had created and formed in the earth. Adam was able to speak out of his mouth the names of the birds, fish, and plants and their identities came to be. Next God establishes that it was not good for man to be alone and so He forms another of his kind to share in partnership the responsibilities for the task at hand. God puts Adam to sleep and pulls from his side the thing that no other man has "the womb". God then forms a body and when Adam awakes he calls her "Wo-man" (the womb of man) and the establishment of partnership was created between man and woman. Adam speaks out of his mouth and names her "Eve" (the first woman). God presents the woman to her mate just as today the bride takes part in the processional down the aisle to meet her soul mate and here God institutes marriage between man and woman. It is through this partnership; through a man and woman that they are to subdue the earth, be fruitful, and multiply. This kingdom purpose still exists today even though the world has tried to institute their own order of relationships by indulging in premarital sex and partaking in same sex relationships; which are considered disgraceful in God's sight.

Don't you realize that those who do wrong will not inherit the Kingdom of God? Don't fool yourselves. Those who indulge in sexual sin, or who worship idols, or commit adultery, or are male prostitutes, or practice homosexuality, or are thieves, or greedy people, or drunkards, or are abusive, or cheat people—none of these will inherit the Kingdom of God."
(I Corinthians 6:9-10 – The Message)

God united man and woman together to subdue the land and work together in partnership to cultivate, nurture, and manage the earth. Many of our issues in the earth today are due to the disconnection of this relationship between man and woman. Thus we have in today's society dysfunctional families. He also commanded that they be fruitful and multiply. It was the institution of marriage as God had planned to be the example of good fruit as man and woman displayed their love for God and each other that others would have the template for living a kingdom life. It was and still is God's plan for man and woman, in the institution of marriage, to also multiply and replenish the earth bringing forth generations.

The Fall and the Redemption

As children we sometimes go against the rules that our parents have established for us. These rules are given in order to keep us on the right path. Yet we oftentimes make decisions that involve "self-gratification" and this leads us in a different direction and can have a lasting affect on our lives. Adam and Eve made the decision to go against the commands of God and because of their decision the place of "paradise" and kingdom living were forever altered.

"At that moment their eyes were opened, and they suddenly felt shame at their nakedness. So they sewed fig leaves together to cover themselves. When the cool evening breezes were blowing, the man and his wife heard the Lord God walking about in the garden. So they hid from the Lord God among the trees. Then the Lord God called to the man, "Where are you?" He replied, "I heard you walking in the garden, so I hid. I was afraid because I was naked."
(Genesis 3:7-10 – KJV)

It was the consequence of man and woman to partake of that which was forbidden that resulted in bondage for all of mankind. Even though man, for many years to come, would do great things for God he was still bound by Adam and Eve's actions.

It is also here we as a human race are introduced to the emotion of FEAR.

And he said, I heard thy voice in the garden, and I was afraid, because I [was] naked; and I hid myself. And he said, Who told thee that thou [wast] naked? Hast thou eaten of the tree, whereof I commanded thee that thou shouldest not eat? (Genesis 3:10-11 KJV)

If you are honest with yourself how many times has fear prevented you from moving forward in your career, family, and even ministry? The adversary is the creator of this emotion and he uses it to lock you up, and blind you from seeing the truth. Know this today; you no longer are bound and fear has "NO CONTROL" over you! It is through your confession that you are a believer in Jesus Christ that now gives you the "Power and Authority" to have dominion over every circumstance and situation in your life and because of the death and resurrection of Jesus Christ He has made you free!

And ye shall know the truth, and the truth shall make you free. (John 8:32)

Kingdom Man
Ambassador Wade

Life in the World of Fairy Tales

We know fairy tales to be described as a fictional story that begins in a place far away and most of the time ends in a place of happily ever after. These stories usually take us through the twists and turns of the character's life but eventually the story ends in their favor.

Several years ago Anita Baker sang a song entitled Fairy tales and the lyrics began with a story her mother told her at bedtime.

Most girls have heard bedtime stories that are designed to give them sweet dreams and also a beautiful fantasy of life ahead.

In Anita Baker's song the lyrics that say… "she never said that we would curse, cry, and scream and lie. She never said that maybe, someday he'd say goodbye...".

There are some days in my life I can relate to these fairy tales. I can relate to the ones I heard growing up and I can also relate to the song sang by Anita Baker.

Imagine how great it would be if the choices we make could be so crystal clear, just like in some of the fairy tale stories we read…if it were only that simple. As you read these following pages about living the life of a Kingdom Man and Kingdom Woman you will understand what I mean…are we really living fairytale lives in this world we call "reality"?

Have you ever wondered what it would be like if we knew what God's choices were for our lives? Sometimes for me it seems as if I go through stage after stage not really knowing which way to turn next. And just like Dorothy, it seems as if we get caught up in a vicious whirlwind, landing us in unfamiliar places, faced with all different kinds of signs and signals that are suppose to give us direction, but "what is the right direction" I ask this question to myself, do you?

Then there are times when life seems to be going fairly smoothly but then the Big Bad Wolf comes into our situations huffing and puffing trying to destroy our house and everything around us too. He's clever with all kinds of tricks up his sleeve. Has he ever tried to trick you with that big red shiny apple? Or with a deal that's just too good to be true? He makes the bad things look good, and we fall for them every time often reacting before we think rather than thinking before we react. It's all a trick to throw us off track.

The bible says in John 10:10 "The robber comes only to steal and to kill and to destroy. I came so they might have life, a great full life."

Sometimes it seems as if the Big Bad Wolf just shows up to surprise us and he's ready to take all that we've worked for, all that we've ever dreamed of and he's trying to destroy us in the process. But there is good news. For Christ came to give us life; a full life, an abundant life.

THY KINGDOM COME

Once Upon A Time

The stories usually begin with “once upon a time”. Some little girls grow up dreaming about the knight in shining armor who would sweep them off their feet and they live happily ever after. Even some little boys grow up dreaming about being rich, famous, and claiming the prettiest girl of them all. Believe it or not we can have these very same fairy tale dreams and so much more, if we just wait patiently on God. Wait patiently on God to transform us from silly, childlike school girls to virtuous women of God and from contrite, hard-headed little boys to men of integrity. And when He is ready, He will present us to our soul mate with all things working out for the good.

The Bible declares that when a man finds a wife, he has found a good thing. Men of God you are a blessing to the treasure you find. You were not made to compete with her but to compliment her as you walk with God’s wisdom. You help to transform that spoiled and sometimes controlling baby girl into the woman of God she was made to be and then both of you can soar together in God’s loving arms living a life of dominion, power, and authority. So, the next question maybe how do we get to this place of the happily ever after? In our fairy tale stories whatever happened to Prince Charming? What ever happened to Cinderella? What ever happened to Snow White? And what about that Knight in shining armor?

THY KINGDOM COME

So, Where's the Knight in Shining Armor?

What about the "Knight in Shining Armor"? Does he only exist in fairy tales, or simply in our dreams? Will he show up driving a Jaguar or a Lamborghini or simply on a pale white horse? Is he a business man, a college graduate or is he a hardworking man, perhaps a trash collector or even a postal worker? Is he a strong, Godly man who understands who he is and his divine purpose?

Every little girl and every little boy have all heard stories that involve a knight in shining armor. Each of us has our own idea of a knight in shining armor. The knight who has dazzles everyone he encounters by exemplifying all those true knightly qualities– (faith, trust, honor, loyalty only to name a few). He always manages to endure every battle and emerge victoriously with his values, integrity and ethics all in tact. He is never overthrown by life's tribulations or temptations. The knight always comes out on top of the world…or at least in our fairy tales.

No little girl dreams of her life with a man any less than a handsome knight and no little boy dreams that he will be defeated by the fire-breathing dragon!

Somewhere in between the little girl's dreams and the day she finds herself bitter and alone something happened. Somewhere between the little boy's dream of being a fireman and the day he becomes the father to two babies by two different women something happens. The fairy tale fades. The dream gets blurry.

THY KINGDOM COME

What happens to the men who never become a knight? What happens to the men whose fairy tale fades away?

I believe we all know these men. We encounter them every day. These men have turned into someone else. They started out wanting to grow up and become knights in shining armor but along the way they dropped out of the program. Some of them have learned a few of the knight's lessons but they haven't quite made it to graduation. Let's meet some of the men who dropped out of Knight Academy. Let's meet the Mr. Wrongs.

Mr. Wrongs

Mr. Bashful

Mr. Bashful is shy, timid, reserved and oftentimes reserved. Mr. Bashful has a difficult time standing up for himself. He finds excuses to avoid situations that involve confrontation. Mr. Bashful never wants to socialize with the family/friends of his mate. He excuses his behavior by saying, "I just want to be with you." On the surface Mr. Bashful seems "deep" or sensitive. This draws women to Mr. Bashful until they soon realize that he is neither. He is simply, Mr. Wrong.

Mr. Doc

Mr. Doc knows everything about every subject. He is very vocal and quick to express his opinions. Doc can sometimes be very forceful and he always lets everyone in the room know what degree he has or where he currently works.

Mr. Doc controls every conversation, answers every question and nobody else will ever get a word in edgewise. Doc always interrupts you, talks loudly and judges everything and everyone around him. The one thing Mr. Doc never talks about is his feelings. Mr. Doc is actually very insecure. He won't talk about his feelings because he has spent years covering up his insecurities with information. Mr. Doc is actually a scared little boy who is afraid that if you ever truly saw him, you wouldn't like him. Mr. Doc is that wrong man.

Mr. Dopey

Mr. Dopey is silly, carefree, and lighthearted He has a great a sense of humor and he uses it, most of the time, to cover up everything else. Mr. Dopey has no desire to be the man in charge. He is rarely serious about anything but jokes about everything. Women fall for Mr. Dopey because every girl wants a man who can make her laugh. Mr. Dopey is the wrong man because although he will make you laugh, the time will come when you need a man to get serious about life. Mr. Dopey has no plans to ever get serious. He will never commit to a woman or anything else.

Mr. Grumpy

Mr. Grumpy is irritable, cranky, ill-tempered, grouchy, complaining, and just plain crabby most of the time. Mr. Grumpy likes to see things running his way. He is disagreeable and often answers every question with a harsh, "no." Mr. Grumpy is the one to burst every bubble and rain on every Sunday day. He always sees the glass as empty even when it is half full. He always gives the negative and never sees the positive. He is quick to tell anyone who will listen about his hard knocks and how life will never get any better.

Women are sometimes attracted to Mr. Grumpy because they hope they will eventually love him enough to bring out his softer, vulnerable side. A woman foolishly thinks Mr. Grumpy reminds her of her father. Mr. Grumpy is nothing like your father. He is the wrong man.

Mr. Happy

Mr. Happy is joyful, cheerful, in high spirits, and appears to always be on cloud nine. Mr. Happy is very likable, warm, and energetic; the life of the party and, everybody just loves him. Mr. Happy seems to be very supportive, and eager to help out with anything. Mr. Happy has a bright smile for everyone and he's most agreeable. In fact, he agrees with everybody. Women and men are a little apprehensive when it comes to Mr. Happy. His sexuality has come into question. Sometimes people wonder if he's really that happy. Is he gay? Is he a down low brother? He's a little bit too happy. The truth of the matter is, Mr. Happy has no spine. He has no backbone and no genuine thoughts of his own. He is quite content to agree with everybody. He will never make a decision on his own and his mind can be changed with the blowing of the wind. Mr. Happy will make you very unhappy. Mr. Happy is another, wrong man.

Mr. Sleepy

Mr. Sleepy is always sleepy. He's tired, lethargic, sluggish, and never wants to do anything. Mr. Sleepy is unresponsive at times, especially when it came to your needs. He is boring, and a daydreamer. He is quick to tell you what he "was going to do" or what he "thought about doing". Mr. Sleepy is quick to tell you why he's so tired. For Mr. Sleepy is a hardworking man. He works hard for the money or so he tells everybody. In fact, Mr. Sleepy works the same amount of hours as anyone else. Usually he works less because Mr. Sleepy is always looking for a way to get over. He gets over on his boss by allowing others to do his work. He gets over on his family because he can never be depended on to do anything. He even gets over on his woman. Mr. Sleepy is lazy. A life with Mr. Sleepy includes the woman doing all the work while Mr. Sleepy relaxes on the couch or in his favorite chair. Mr. Sleepyy is no knight in shining armor. He's much too tired for that.

These are the wrong men who have no place in your fairy tale. Is there such a thing as a Knight in Shining Armor? Is there a man who is able to emerge triumphantly through all of life's battles or is this simply another fairy tale? Do fairy tales ever come true? Will women ever find their Knight in shining armor or is it just a pipe dream? Will men ever wear the suit of armor and handsomely ride in to arrive at that magical place of happily ever after?

Yes, there are some men who endure life's twists and turns and still come out on top. These men of God are totally sold out and devoted to being the men that God would have them to be. He's a man who thinks of his Kingdom Woman as a priceless gift that is worth the wait and willing to treat her like HIS QUEEN! He's the man who will sweep her off your feet before she ever realizes she's left the ground.

Mr. Right – The Kingdom Man

Let's take a closer look at our knights. What makes his armor shine?

In medieval times when a knight needed to protect himself in battle he would wear shining armor, confident that the protective gear would keep him from injury or even death. He wore this heavy steel armor that shined like new money and he took great pride knowing he was able to conquer the impending battle. After each battle his armor all scoffed, dented and mutilated only to be repair by the smith for the next quest. But underneath that armor who was the man? Did he really ever get damaged from the battle? Was he left with scars? Did the armor really protect him?

In life's battles we expect to recover quickly from our scars, bruises and our pain. There are times when we are injured in battle. There are times when we don't recover as quickly as we think we should. This would make the average man feel hopeless. The Kingdom man, however, recognizes and acknowledges that even when he does his best - there are going to be circumstances, results, and people he can't control. A Kingdom Man, much like the knight in shining armor, puts on his armor. The Kingdom Man puts on the whole armor of God. He is a humble man acknowledging he is still under construction. He is fashioned and pressed in the furnace of life.

The Kingdom man knows that his armor is made to be worn at all times and there is no reason to ever take it off. The Kingdom man makes the decision to put on the armor of God, each and everyday. He knows the armor has been formed, fitted, and custom designed just for him by the heavenly armor-maker himself.

Use every piece of God's armor to resist the enemy in the time of evil, so that after the battle you will still be standing firm. Stand your ground, putting on the sturdy belt of truth and the body armor of God's righteousness. For shoes, put on the peace that comes from the Good News, so that you will be fully prepared. In every battle you will need faith as your shield to stop the fiery arrows aimed at you by Satan. Put on salvation as your helmet, and take the sword of the Spirit, which is the word of God. Pray at all times and on every occasion in the power of the Holy Spirit. Stay alert and be persistent in your prayers for all Christians everywhere. (Ephesians 6:13-18 - NLT)

A Kingdom Man knows he is God's chosen vessel and because of this he has to be prepared for battle at all times. The Kingdom man puts on his armor every morning knowing that God has prepared him for battle.

He first puts on ***breastplate of righteousness***:

The Kingdom Man begins his day in submission to God. He goes into battle understanding that he is a righteous man through Christ. He is good and of moral character. His character defines him as a man. Nothing ever takes him out of his character. His character was defined by God. There is a purpose to his life and he knows it. He understands it and he lives by it. This breastplate of righteousness is placed firmly over his heart. He guards his heart knowing his heart breathes life.

For shoes he puts on ***the peace that comes from the Good News***. This ensures he is fully prepared. The good news is the Gospel of Christ. The Kingdom Man studies his word. He studies the plan book. He is equipped in the word of God knowing this is his only defense against any enemy. He studies the bible so that he knows God. This is his preparation for any battle and any enemy.

In every battle a Kingdom Man needs ***his faith as his shield***. A Kingdom Man knows his faith is the thing that stops the enemy in his tracks.

What is faith? It is the confident assurance that what we hope for is going to happen. It is the evidence of things we cannot yet see. (Hebrews 11:1 – NLT)

The Kingdom man stands on every promise God has given him in His Word. His faith is in God and God alone. As God's ambassador in this world, the Kingdom man acknowledges each battle is part of God's plan. He knows that every day he will be attacked by darts of opposition, discouragement and fear will try to flood his mind; but his shield of faith is what he uses to protect himself.

The Kingdom Man then puts put on salvation as his ***helmet.***

The "Kingdom Man" wears the helmet of Salvation. His helmet protects his head – his mind. Because he has a relationship with God, his mind is filled with the things of God. His desire is to do the will of God and his mind is constantly overflowing with the belief "I can do all things through Christ which strengthens me." The Kingdom Man has a strong mind. His mind is fixed on his mission. His mission is to please God.

Finally, the Kingdom Man understands he must ***pray at all times and on every occasion***. The Kingdom Man knows his only line of communication with his God is through his prayer life. The Kingdom man has a prayer life that includes daily prayer to God for himself and his fellow man. He is truthful about his shortcomings and is never boastful as he works toward God's glory. The Kingdom man is truthful concerning all things and he stands on the word of God. The Kingdom Man is not concerned about his battle. He knows that God will always make a way out of trouble for him.

However, the good news is that "God is faithful, who will not suffer you to be tempted (whether it be doubting or giving up) above that ye are able; but will with the temptation also make a way to escape, that ye may be able to bear it." (I Corinthians 10:13 (NKJV)

There's no bashful, grumpy, happy, sleepy man here. No…here is the right man. Here is the Kingdom Man.

THY KINGDOM COME

Who is He?

- A Kingdom man is able to catch his mate in the Spirit realm right before the fall.

- A Kingdom man thinks clearly and is always striving to do better; he is always in search of what God has in store for him.

- A Kingdom man is a man of his word. He says what he means and means what he says. His word is his bond. He is dependable and reliable.

- A Kingdom man is sensitive and caring. He is encouraging, compassionate and understanding in all of his relationships.

- A Kingdom man is grounded in the word of God, and no mistake about it… he knows that he knows that he knows… that Jesus is Lord.

- A Kingdom man isn't insecure when it comes to his woman and who she is. He is her greatest supporter and biggest fan.

- A Kingdom man will find a virtuous woman and take great pride in her. One of his greatest attribute is making sure his Kingdom Woman (WIFE) shines.

• A Kingdom man is passionate and overflowing with the enthusiasm for life and readily accepts change knowing that even in change, God is still in control.

• The Kingdom man is quick to listen and slow to speak.

So, men of God if you dropped out of the Knight's academy, it's time to enroll in the Kingdom Man's academy instead. It's time to take your rightful place inside God's kingdom…you are a Kingdom Man.

◇◇◇◇◇◇◇◇◇◇◇◇◇◇◇◇◇◇◇◇◇◇◇◇◇◇◇◇◇◇◇◇◇◇◇◇◇

Do You Want to Know the Truth?

Women of God, have you ever passed up the one? Yes ladies, men are all around us. We pass them on the streets, in the malls, and at work and it could be possible that we've passed up the Kingdom Man because we don't know what a "Kingdom Man" really looks like. Many times he's not flashy or rich which can be some of the characteristics that would catch our attention. He might not wear a suit or cruise in a Bentley. He might not have a body like Hercules or have a smile like Denzel Washington.

Here's the truth...wouldn't you'd rather find someone who's got your back rather than someone who makes your head turn? Understand that later in life the looks fade away, gravity affects the body, and you discover you need a Godly man. A man of God who is walking in wisdom through the trials and tribulations of life.

THY KINGDOM COME

This is the man who will hold you and the family up every step of the way. What you're really looking for is a relationship and not a situation.

All relationships work best when they are ordered by God. We have to come to the realization that God knows what and who is best for us. I also believe sometimes we push the good ones aside because they don't fit our profile and many times that Kingdom man was right within arms length and we let him slip right through our fingers.

When I was in the world my ideal guy was a man in uniform and a little rough around the edges. He had to be tall, handsome, and intelligent. He had to be someone who had a 5-year plan and was making steps toward achieving his goals in life. He had to be a romantic who would sweep me off my feet, wine and dine me at the finest of restaurants because I deserved nothing but the best. My perfect man had to add to my equation, bring more than average to the table and keep up with my maintenance. I wanted someone who was sweet, had common interests, a good conversationalist and would spoil me like a princess. I've always been a daydreamer and optimist. But when I entered into adulthood reality showed its true colors and I know I'm not alone you've been there too. The men we fantasized about were not always the right ones for us. Who do we really want on our endless wish list? Is it the one you're trying to mold together yourself? A little of this one and a little of that one and when we pull him all together you have a "hot mess" of man. And it is this mess we continue to get in our relationships over and over again the same drama, the same song and dance.

THY KINGDOM COME

I remember a few years back having a conversation with a girlfriend. She shared with me what she thought a Kingdom Man should look like. She realized over the years her standards had changed quite a bit. Yes, she still wanted someone who was tall, handsome and intelligent but now she discovered that just those things didn't make the man. A Kingdom Man was so much more than what he appeared to be on the outside.

We both agreed the most important things we wanted in man was for him to be totally sold out and devoted to God. He should possess unconditional love just as Christ has unconditional love for the church. Our ideal men would have the heart, mind, and the love of Jesus. As we continued our conversation we had unknowingly described the traits and qualities of a Kingdom Man. It was this man who would fulfill very item on our shopping list and even some items we hadn't even considered. We concluded our conversation celebrating the fact that yes, this kind of man does exist. Even though he may have his shortcomings, imperfections, and drawbacks he is out there. There is a Kingdom Man who God designed just for us. He would be our delectable cake with all our favorite toppings…We had finally identified Mr. Right.

But what about you, woman of God? Are you Mrs. Right? Can the Kingdom Man find you? Are you a Kingdom Woman? Are you what God says when he calls for a "good thing"?

Women of God, if you are in search of a Kingdom Man have no fear, God is able. The only thing you need to do is make sure you are available when he finds you. For the bible says…a man who finds a wife finds a good thing.

Kingdom Woman
Ambassador Wade

Mirror, Mirror on the Wall

"Mirror, mirror on the wall who is...."

We've all said it, heard it, and even read the bedtime story but what is so profound about the whole thing is we've all probably stood in a mirror and said, "Mirror, Mirror on the Wall Who is the..." Then we stopped. We each have a different question to ask the mirror. We asked who's the prettiest, smartest, best, most ambitious, most likely to succeed, and so on.

Several months ago, I had the pleasure of hearing Ambassador Wilson of the renowned Word Kingdom Ministries preach a sermon entitled Mirror, Mirror on the Wall. The message was designed to get you to take an honest look at the image you project to the world as well as to yourself. This message stuck in my head for some time.

I began to ask myself several questions:

"Mirror, mirror on the wall... Am I who I say I am?"
"Mirror, mirror on the wall... Who do others say I am?"
"Mirror, mirror on the wall...Am I a Kingdom Woman?"

THY KINGDOM COME

Please understand, now I know who I am but it hasn't been that way always. I grew up thinking that my life was ok, and wherever I was at the present time was where I suppose to be. I guess I really never gave it much thought. Throughout my life I was defined by the man I was dating, the family I was born into, the church I attended and the like. It was the life I was dealt and I was playing the hand. No one called me a "Kingdom Woman" and never explained to me what a kingdom woman was.

But then one day I read this scripture:

"Well," they replied, "some say John the Baptist, some say Elijah, and others say Jeremiah or one of the other prophets. Then he asked them, "But who do you say I am?"

Simon Peter answered, "You are the Messiah, the Son of the living God." Matthew 16: 14-16 (NLV)

I read this scripture over and over again and I began to ask myself just as Jesus questioned the disciples…who do they say I am?

We go through life trying to find out who we are and what God has called us to be. Through test and trials, skills and talents, likes and dislikes sometimes it hard to find the passion and discover the true calling of God.

I've discovered through the years we don't necessarily walk as a Kingdom Woman because we don't know what a Kingdom Woman looks like. We've never been taught to live a life as a Kingdom

THY KINGDOM COME

Woman, sometimes we feel that it would take too much of our time and effort to develop this lifestyle, or simply we're just a afraid.

Most women are just like I was. Going through life allowing whatever happens in our lives to define us. We try to become like other people or we search in all the wrong places looking for ourselves. We have all been guilty of allowing situations and circumstances to define us instead of allowing God and the word of God to define us. It is only when stumble upon something that opens our eyes and then one day we find ourselves looking in the mirror of our lives which causes us to ask and seek God for some answers.

It happened one day during my study time when I stumbled on this scripture in Psalms 139:

Oh yes, you shaped me first inside, then out;
you formed me in my mother's womb.
I thank you, High God—you're breathtaking!
Body and soul, I am marvelously made!
I worship in adoration—what a creation!
You know me inside and out,
you know every bone in my body;
You know exactly how I was made, bit by bit,
how I was sculpted from nothing into something.
Like an open book, you watched me grow
from conception to birth;
all the stages of my life were spread out before you,
The days of my life all prepared
before I'd even lived one day.
(Psalms 139:13-16 - The Message)

THY KINGDOM COME

This passage of scripture caused me to understand that it's no mystery who I am. There is no need to wander aimlessly through life. God had a plan for my life before he formed me in my mother's womb. Long before my father ever had thoughts of my mother, God had already decided who I would become. He planned what I would look like, act like and most importantly, what I would walk like. It is here that I began to use the keys that would unlock the doors toward my transformation in becoming a Kingdom woman.

I can say that my life at times has felt like a hallway with many doors to choose from but it was these keys that helped me get closer toward discovering who I really was and maybe these keys can help you too.

Kingdom Keys:

- **Identify the Kingdom Woman**
  Recognize, classify, and discover just who you are.

- **Taking control over your life**
  Manage, organize, take charge of, run, and have power over yourself.

- **Practice being a Kingdom Woman daily**
  Uncover the woman you are within you. Prepare by studying the Word of God daily. Stop doing the same old routines and start walking in your new life.

- **Surrender, Stand, and Give Him Praise**
  Give Him your all. Praise Him for what He has done and never turn back but continue to move forward. Never surrender to the ways of the world but stand firm in God's plan and purpose for your life.

It's Time for a Transformation--The Stages

Every Woman is a princess to the Master. As we blossom from princess little girls to Kingdom women, God knows the plans He has for our lives. It's time to transform yourself into what God desires for your life. I believe there are three phases that every woman goes through. I call them the stages of transformation.

Ugly Duckling - The stage where you realized you were different from everyone else. You looked and acted differently from others around you.

You were born in a normal family where your life was just as normal as the next. Maybe you did look a little different from your other siblings or maybe there was something distinguishing about you that became more and more noticeable. The other children weren't as dark as you. Other little girls had straighter hair than your hair. You were skinny or maybe you were a little chubby girl. You didn't notice it much at first but then one day you noticed that everybody seemed to make a distinction between you and other little girls. Everyone seemed to notice this difference in you. You grow a few more years and realize you have developed a bit of a complex about the thing that makes your different.

THY KINGDOM COME

What do we do when we have a complex? We try to hide it. We try to mask it. We try to cover it with makeup or clothes. We try to fix it and pretend we're just like everyone else. But the truth of the matter is you're not like everyone else. You are different. There is something distinctly different about you. No matter how you try to hide it you are different.

Somewhere in life you learn to deal with being different don't you? That thing that used to be wrong now seems to be right. If we're honest with ourselves, usually some man makes it okay for us. A man says, "You have beautiful eyes." He might say, "Your dark skin glistens in the moonlight." Maybe you heard, "You are lean and sleek like a model." It sure beats the days when they called you string bean doesn't it?

Someone shines a light on the thing that made you feel inferior and now you're feeling good about yourself. You then learn that it's okay to be different. You begin to fall in love with what could be you. You fall in love with someone else's image of you. You started off being an ugly duckling and now you're starting to blossom into a beautiful swan.

We have to remember that beauty isn't what we put on, it's not in make-up, jewelry and clothes we wear. Our beauty is in our obedience to God. True beauty never fades with age, it shines because of the love we have on the inside for Him and it will never die.

Cinderella - This stage is where you try to live up to the fantasy of others. You do everything in your power to make someone else believe you can be a princess.

In the fairy tale, Cinderella was treated badly, but she never mistreated others around her. She cleaned. She cooked. She did everything trying to please people who should have loved her. Women are nurturers by design. Therefore, we innately want to do for others. We instinctively want to make those around us feel loved. Cinderella spends years trying to make others love her. She tries to please everybody. Then one day a prince enters the picture and Cinderella begins to dream. She dreams of being in love. She dreams of the day when a man will worship and adore her. Much like the fairy tale Cinderella, you long for the day when you will be allowed to wear a beautiful white gown and waltz down the isle to your awaiting prince charming.

" The man who finds a wife finds a treasure, and he receives favor from the Lord. (Proverbs 18:21-23 – NLT)

The fairy tale of Cinderella ends when the prince arrives with a missing shoe that fits the abused and mistreated Cinderella perfectly. They go on to live…happily ever after.

Can you see the Cinderella in your mirror? Cinderella can you see your transformation as God turns your pumpkin into a limo, a rat into your driver. He then turns your rags into designer originals, your flip flops into an awesome pair of glass slippers.

One day I had to realize that God had those same shoes for me. In God's eyes I am a Cinderella too and I have shoes that are "Designer Originals" designed by God himself. These shoes are just for me and only my feet can fill them no matter who else tries them on no one can wear them like I can.

Woman of God let me be the first to tell you. There is a "shoe" that fits you perfectly. It was designed for you and only for you. That shoe is called *purpose*. It is yours and yours alone. Unlike Cinderella, no prince charming will come for you with your purpose in his hand. Your purpose comes from the hand of God and to find it you must first find Him.

Our lives are in his hands, and he keeps our feet from stumbling. (Psalm 66:8-10 – NLT)

Find Him and you'll find your perfect slipper. Find Him and you'll find your purpose. Your life is in His hand.

Dorothy – (The Wizard of Oz) – In this stage every woman finds herself living in a place that is foreign to her. She's accepted Jesus as her Lord and Savior, now what? She's growing up and beginning to discover her purpose. But now what? There's a part of her that clearly understands she is destined to be a Kingdom Woman but much like Dorothy in the fairy tale, she's not comfortable in her new place.

"Toto, I've got a feeling we're not in Kansas any more. We must be over the rainbow!"

THY KINGDOM COME

In discovering your purpose you will for a while, find yourself in a lonely, unfamiliar place. Something about it feels right, yet there are some things that feels very wrong. Much like Dorothy you want to leave this new place. You're happy about your purpose but you don't like this place you're in. Many women on the road to becoming a Kingdom Woman have had to leave things and people behind. There may be seasons in your life where you have to leave your mother, father or family members. You may have to leave behind some cherished friends. You may even have to walk away from your beloved career.

And Jesus replied, "I assure you that everyone who has given up house or brothers or sisters or mother or father or children or property, for my sake and for the Good News, will receive now in return, a hundred times over, houses, brothers, sisters, mothers, children, and property-with persecutions. And in the world to come they will have eternal life. (Mark 10:29-30 ~ NLT)

Now, here you stand in a foreign place feeling lost, and all you have is a promise from God that it will get better. You begin to travel down an unfamiliar road hoping, searching for something better. Searching for a time when you will feel comfortable again. Searching for a place that feels remotely like…home.

Like Dorothy we're traveling on an unfamiliar road headed toward Emerald City the place they say has all the answer for our happiness. But as a Kingdom woman we're not looking for "Kansas" or the Emerald City but we're trying to find our way back to God.

Through this journey we encounter so many disappointments and pain leaving us sometimes so confused.

In Dorothy's story she had a host of friends and enemies, from the munchkins to the wizard and even the wicked witch. All trying to show her the way home or setting traps every step of the way. We too have these same kinds of friends and enemies. Those who are trying to help make life easier as we travel but also those that the adversary puts in our path to try and make us stumble or give up. So as we're going down this yellow brick road, this place the world calls the road to success, we must ask ourselves, "is this right road? Is this the road I should be on?"

Along the way, much like Dorothy, you encounter some new friends. And believe it or not just like you, your friends are confused too. You make a fine group together don't you? Every woman has at least one friend who seems to be missing what grandma calls, "common sense". This friend quickly latches on to you because even though you're lost, you do have a brain. You're smart enough to know that something's missing in your life. So you and your new friend travel down the road of life together searching. Next you may encounter someone who's looking for his heart; someone looking for love and you offer to help. Even though you're lost you do understand everybody needs love. This new friend may come in the form of a boyfriend or love interest. Don't be confused, though, this is no Kingdom Man. He's one of the people who enters your life after you're finished with all the wrong men but before you are found by your Kingdom Man. You may also encounter a new friend who seems a little afraid. In fact, this new friend is scared of everything and everybody. Your friend lacks courage. She knows she has a purpose too but she's afraid to do anything about it. Your new friend quickly offers to go along on your journey with you, hoping she may find some courage to pursue her own dreams.

You and your new friends are on your way. But where? You're traveling down the road searching, searching, searching but where are you going and what are you searching for?

The only person who really knows is the Great I Am. God himself. There is no need to consult the psychic or use tarot cards to help us with directions because God instructs us daily.

Dorothy was trying to find Kansas in the same way, and the Kingdom Woman is searching too. The Kingdom Woman is in pursuit of something greater...she is looking for "GOD".

Every day she arises to speak with her heavenly Father for the directions of the day to direct her path.

Remember, Dorothy asked everybody she encountered for directions. You are a lot like Dorothy in this respect. You will ask anyone for help except the One who can help you. You spend season after season asking questions of the people around you or people who are no better off than you. Finally, one day you find yourself at a place you thought would make everything okay. You find yourself in front of the great and powerful wizard. Your wizard might be a person, place or thing. It could be that beautiful house you longed for. It could be the man you thought would make everything alright if he'd just marry you. Your wizard could be the title of Vice President or C.E.O. Your wizard could be the degree you struggled to obtain. But whatever your wizard, you find that it doesn't fulfill you. It doesn't make you happy. Your life is still quite empty. You've achieved the things you thought would make you happy and now you find that you're still not fulfilled and satisfied. You spend countless hours at church week after week. You're on committees and volunteering in your community but you're still not there yet. You should be happy. On the outside it appears that you've got it all but you know the truth. You're still searching. You don't have love, peace or joy. You've traveled down this long road and you're empty, tired and you still haven't found…home.

"Are you tired? Worn out? Burned out on religion? Come to me. Get away with me and you'll recover your life. I'll show you how to take a real rest. Walk with me and work with me—watch how I do it. Learn the unforced rhythms of grace. I won't lay anything heavy or ill-fitting on you. Keep company with me and you'll learn to live freely and lightly." (Matthew 11:28-30 ~ The Message)

At the end of the fairy tale Dorothy had been searching for home and finally realized home was in her heart. All she had to do was believe. All she had to do was make a choice to believe and then she could go home.

As a Kingdom Woman, you have a choice. Do you want to live an empty, unfulfilled life or do you want to live life and live it more abundantly? The answers to your life are inside of you. There is no magic trick, no secret prayer and there is no one else who can make you a Kingdom Woman. Unlike Dorothy, you don't need magic slippers! All a Kingdom Woman needs to do is…walk. Your ruby-red slippers are the blood of Jesus. He called you into this life and destined you to be a Kingdom Woman. You simply have to choose. You've spent years practicing, transitioning, imitating others. Now the dress rehearsal is over. You are in full costume and makeup. You have all the props, scenery, and the spotlight is on you. You are the star of this show. It's time to walk out onto the stage of life and be a Kingdom Woman!

A Kingdom Woman is a Royal Priestess

A woman of God, a royal priestess, a virtuous woman is known not by the clothes she wears or the car she drives. She is marked by this aura and the way she carries herself. First and foremost, a woman of God is in love with the true lover of her soul before any man. She is in love with Jesus Christ. She knows that she needs no man to complete her for Christ left nothing out when he created her. She exemplifies strength, patience and wisdom in her daily walk that always seems unique. She doesn't define herself by the world's standards of what a great woman is, but by the principles and the values found within the word of God. She seeks to please God and not the world. She is graceful and beautiful whether slim or thick, dark or light, for she knows her true value is more than skin deep.

A Kingdom Woman – Who Is She?

- A Kingdom Woman is worth far more than the most exquisite diamonds and she knows her worth.

- A Kingdom Woman is trustworthy, honest and sincere.

- A Kingdom Woman treats her husband generously and lovingly until death does them part.

- A Kingdom Woman is loving and forgiving in everything she does.

- A Kingdom Woman is a business woman. She manages her home and her career with excellence.

- A Kingdom Woman is money savvy. She spends wisely and saves much more than she spends.

- A Kingdom Woman is disciplined and organized. She is always prepared for anything life throws her way.

- A Kingdom Woman has a special relationship with God. She spends quality time with her Lord and Savior.

- A Kingdom woman is rooted in the word of God and seeks God for everything she does. She is a good and virtuous woman.

THY KINGDOM COME

Many women have done wonderful things, but you've outclassed them all!" Charm can mislead and beauty soon fades. The woman to be admired and praised is the woman who lives in the Fear-of-God. Give her everything she deserves! Festoon her life with praises! (Proverbs 31:29-31 – The Message)

Kingdom Marriage
The Ambassadors

Marriage…for better, for worst, for richer, for poorer, in sickness and in health, to love and cherish till death do us part. These are the promises that we make that begin the covenant of marriage that we are all familiar with. In this section of the book you will find our joint perspectives on marriage. Since we are all unique, individual creations, God has blessed each person with a unique ministry of marriage. Our purpose here is not to have you emulate our views, but instead, to help you define your own perfect ministry of marriage. Every Adam is created differently and so is every Eve.

There are four key principles of a successful Kingdom Marriage:

1. Cleave
2. Singleness
3. Joint Heirs
4. The Mirror Image

Ambassador A. Wilson:

When my husband and I married, I was in love. People marry for all sorts of reasons. Some marry for companionship; some marry for money, social status, etc. I married for one reason. Love! I was so in love with this man I could tell when he walked in a room. Long before he spoke a word I knew he was there. I could feel his presence. He was the first man I'd ever known to keep his word. If he said he was going to call, he called. If he said he was going to show up, by golly, he showed up! We had been great friends before marriage and I knew we'd be even greater friends after marriage.

We got engaged after one year of dating. We were engaged that September and were married in December of the same year. He didn't want to wait to start our new life together and neither did I.

In Genesis Chapter 2 we find God establishing marriage. God said, "it is not good for the man to be alone; I will make him a help meet." God then performs the first medical surgery on Adam where he took one of Adam's ribs and formed Eve. When I got married, I knew I had the rib of my husband in my side. I felt a kinship with him. We were so in love we made other people "sick" with our mushiness. We foolishly thought this feeling would last forever. Now don't get me wrong, we're still very much in love. But the butterflies in the stomach and the feeling that overtook me whenever he walked into a room were just that…feelings. And feelings change don't they? The lovesick puppies grew up and had to learn to deal with life's issues. We had to learn to deal with our differences.

The bible says, "therefore shall a man leave his father and his mother, and shall cleave unto his wife: and they shall be one flesh." *(Genesis 2:24 –KJV)*

This was my first mistake in marriage:

First Things First: Cleave

My husband had a severe case of the Popeye/Olive Oyl Syndrome or P.O.O.S as I affectionately like to call it and I had a huge case of "My Father Knows Best" (MFKB). Things sailed along fine for while in our marriage but after a period of time, things hit the fan. After a few years our severe "illnesses" took their toll on the marriage. At one point I felt like my husband was rescuing every woman but me. He was always running to help somebody with some problem. They'd call in the middle of the night and he'd race from our bed to help out a relative in distress. It was like Popeye rescuing Olive Oyl after she had been in a dispute with Bluto. Time after time Olive Oyl would scream, Popeye would eat his spinach and off he'd go. Only I'd be left alone to watch my beloved Popeye rush off to rescue someone else.

My husband, on the other hand, had his own set of issues with me and my lack of ability to cleave. He was being made to go up against my father in every way. Here, my new husband was being put side by side in comparison to my Christian father who had been married to my mother for nearly 40 years and had already raised three children.

Time and time again I'd say, "My daddy doesn't do that" or "You should call my dad and ask him what to do". It would be years before my husband and I would discussed how he felt about my Father Knows Best disease and I about his Popeye/Olive Oyl Syndrome. Therefore, it took a time long before we learned how to cleave to one another.

In fact, it would be nearly four years into the marriage as I was preparing a sermon for Women's Day event that I realized my own lack of cleaving. It suddenly dawned on me that my father was the perfect husband…for my mother. I repented to God and my husband and learned to cleave to my husband just before the first birthday of our daughter.

Let's define what the word cleave means so that we clearly understand what it means as it relates to a Kingdom Marriage. The bible says a man must leave his father and mother and cleave to his wife. The very life and fullness of your marriage depends on your ability to cleave to one another. This word cleave "means stick to, embrace or to be bound to".

God requires a husband and wife to be bound together in a way that no one can separate them or get in the middle of them. Just as the coils of a strong, solid rope are woven together, the "marriage rope" should withstand and secures any tasks or mission that is required of it. It is only when someone or something purposely unravels this rope will it begin to separate and weaken to the point of destruction. Then the rope is no longer usable. Don't we see this consistently in marriages as people and things unravel the bond between a husband and wife? God wants to strengthen your marriage as tightly as woven rope, making it strong and secure knowing that nothing shall separate what God has joined together.

As a Pastor and Minister, when I've been given the honor of officiating a wedding ceremony, just before I allow the groom to kiss his bride I make a practice of standing between them. I stand between the couple and I advise, "May this be the last time anyone comes between you." And I then allow the groom to salute his new bride with a kiss.

Inside your marriage, you must learn to lean and depend on one another as if your life depends on it…because in reality, it does. When you are married you are not to cleave to your parents, relatives and friends. Instead you must cleave to your spouse. Yes, you are to take the lessons learned from your parents, but you are not to cleave to them. You are now to embrace your new family.

This leads us right into the next principle which is, Singleness.

Singleness Not Partnership – One Not Two (Two Became One Flesh)

Ambassador T. Walls:

God proclaimed, "and they shall be one flesh".
When a man leaves his father and mother for marriage he then embraces his wife wrapping his arms around her as they become one. Inside a Kingdom Marriage, there are no longer two as they one become one flesh.

Society teaches us that marriage is about two people giving fifty/fifty. You give fifty percent and I give fifty percent and together we make one hundred percent. Yet in most marriages even these percentage still come up short, because each person has not fully committed themselves to this union. In many instances one person ends up making up for the lack of the other and this person is now over taxed, and under appreciated.

Inside a Kingdom Marriage, God designed that the man give one hundred percent of himself, the woman give one hundred percent of herself and they are then able to stand before God as one fully responsible unit. This union where each person gives one hundred percent to the marriage leaves no room for societal views, egos or an enemy of any kind. The husband is fully committed to the union and so is his wife.

The two of them, the Man and his Wife,
were naked, but they felt no shame. (Gen. 2:25)

In a Kingdom Marriage there should be no shame between your relationship with God and your relationship with your mate. As we have shared in the previous chapters (Kingdom Man and Kingdom Woman) it is important to prepare yourself for this time in your life and to make sure there has been a process of self examination, repentance, deliverance and restoration before entering into the ministry of marriage. You must spiritually take the time during your courtship, prior to the marriage, to stand spiritually naked and expose yourself, airing out the issues that you have with yourself and with your future mate. It is vitally important to never enter into this sacred, covenant relationship thinking you will change your mate. God gave us authority over the things of the earth but not over each other. You will never change your mate. Don't fool yourself into thinking things will change after a marriage. There should also be no "secrets" withheld from your mate prior to marriage. Part of being unashamed is being honest enough to admit your faults, insecurities and failures to each other and also accepting each other as is. This is what it takes to be in singleness with your spouse. And when things arise after you make your vows to each other, you must maintain an open line of communication. You are no longer two but now one. If one person is hurting the other person automatically hurts as well. Your relationship is now embroidered with love and honesty so that you have the ability to open up to your mate and expose your true feelings not being ashamed but assured that your partner will not hurt you but will connect with you.

Joint Heirs

Ambassador E. Wade:

When you operate inside a kingdom marriage, God will bless abundantly because kingdom marriage is God's divine plan. It is a covenant relationship. It is a binding contract made between two people and that contract is signed or decreed by God. God desires your marriage to be fruitful, and not just with children but in every way. When you marry, God no longer sees two, he now sees one. In order to receive the fullness of life, you have to operate as one. When you marry and treat each other God's way, you become joint heirs in the blessings of God. God can't bless the husband without blessing the wife. In the same manner, God can't bless the wife without blessing the husband.

1 Peter chapter 3 talks specifically about how husbands and wives must treat one another. God instructs wives to be good wives to your husband, responsive to his needs. He also instructs the same for the husbands, requiring them to be good husbands to their wives honoring and delighting in them. The bible refers to women as the weaker vessel. The Message bible says women lack some of

the advantages of men but in the new life of God's grace, men and women are equals. The scripture ends with a promise. It ends telling the husbands: "treat your wives, then as equals so your prayers don't run aground." (1 Peter 3:7 - The Message)

The King James Version of the bible in the same passage says, 'Likewise, ye husbands, dwell with [them] according to knowledge, giving honor unto the wife, as unto the weaker vessel, and as being heirs together of the grace of life; that your prayers be not hindered." Treating your spouse well insures unhindered prayers. Ain't God good?

The Mirror Image

The Ambassadors:

…But don't just listen to God's word. You must do what it says. Otherwise, you are only fooling yourselves. For if you listen to the word and don't obey, it is like glancing at your face in a mirror. You see yourself, walk away, and forget what you look like. But if you look carefully into the perfect law that sets you free, and if you do what it says and don't forget what you heard, then God will bless you for doing it. *(James 1:22-25 – NLT)*

What do you see when you look at your marriage? Do you see yourself? Do you see your mate? You should see God. And everyone looking at your marriage should see the very face of God. Your marriage should look like Christ loving the church. Your marriage should have love, praise, and worship…all the things that God designed to show his love for the church.

THY KINGDOM COME

Every girl dreams of walking down the aisle in a white dress. Every boy longs for a beautiful wife to share his successful life with. It's called a fairy tale. But what the fairy tale doesn't show you is the real deal. The bride won't wear a beautiful white dress every day and the groom's life isn't successful every single day. There are ups and downs in every marriage. There are good days and there are bad days. But you have to ask yourself on a regular basis, "What do we look like when we look in the mirror?" Does the marriage look like God?

Ephesians Chapter 5 teaches us how to love inside a kingdom marriage. When you find yourselves making a wrong turn in marriage, learn to watch what God does for the church and mimic that behavior. And what do we see Him do throughout the bible as it relates to His people…He loves. God loves us even when we are wrong and He still shows us his best. Out of respect for Christ we must be good to each other inside a kingdom marriage. Wives you must understand and support your husbands in ways that shows your support for Christ. That's what submission is. It's loving your husband God's way. It's surrendering to God's love inside your marriage. When you look in the mirror, wife, do you see yourself supporting your husband in a way that pleases God? Just as the church submits to Christ as the leader of the church, wives must also submit to their husbands.

Husbands, the bible instructs you to go all out in love for your wives, the same way Christ went all out for the church. Your love should be defined by giving. Christ never got anything from the church. That was not his mission. His mission was to give. Now this doesn't say you are in an empty marriage where you are always giving and never getting…quite the contrary. When you give, the laws of God say you will get a greater investment on your return. You will get far more than you gave. Christ gave everything; He gave His very life for the church. The bible instructs husband to do the same. His words evoke his wife's beauty. Everything he does and says is designed to bring out the best in her. And since you are one with your wife, it's really in your best interest isn't it?

Now go back and look in the mirror. Don't you see Christ smiling back at you?

Kingdom Family
Ambassador Wilson

Better than the Huxtables!

From 1984 to 1992 countless families all over America tuned their televisions to NBC to watch The Cosby Show. I know I don't have to remind you Bill Cosby plays a physician who is married to a lawyer and they have five beautiful children. Week after week we watched and fell in love with the fictitious Huxtable family. Each week we laughed and often cheered as they showed us a loving, happy family.

This was a family that all of America could understand. It wasn't a show about an African American family, no; it was a show about a loving family. And no matter what your family situation looked like, all of America longed to be the great Huxtable family.

What if I told you there was a system to having a family even better than the Huxtable family?

Believe it or not, God designed the Kingdom Family to be even better than this fictitious family. Before we begin discussing the benefits and advantages of a Kingdom Family, let's define family!

Family! It Starts in the Bloodline!

What is a family? God's ultimate design for the family began with a man and a woman and his first instructions to that man and woman was to be fruitful and to multiply – meaning have children. But it doesn't always work out that way does it? Sometimes a family is a mother and child. Sometimes a family is a father and his children. Sometimes a family is simply a husband and his wife. Sometimes the people you love and call family are of no biological relation to you at all.

No matter what your family looks like, it's still a family. The definition of a family is two or more people joined together by common ancestry or a group of people who share a bloodline. For Ambassadors the bloodline starts with Jesus Christ. Whomever God has joined you together with through His bloodline is considered to be your family. Family is a bloodline decision made by God.

The Christian definition of a family is a covenant connection between two or more individuals that has been established and predestined by God. Understand clearly that you don't get a choice in who God selects for your family. Even with your church family you didn't choose. It matters not how many people are in your church congregation, it is still destined by God and it is a covenant relationship established by and through Him.

Look at your family. You didn't choose them but they are still apart of you. From your parents all the way down through the cousin nobody wants to talk about. It's still your family designed by God and you have a heart to heart connection with them.

It doesn't matter if you went through a bitter divorce or if you are a widow or widower. It also doesn't matter if you are a "baby daddy" or you find yourself involved in a supreme case of "baby momma drama". The bottom line is you are still a family. Whatever your current marital situation is, or lack thereof, you still have a covenant connection that needs to be honored and respected. You may be divorced and have children with your ex-wife. God still expects you as an ambassador to honor the covenant relationship established by Him. You are still to honor and respect the covenant of that relationship.

Isn't it funny to watch the church family? You could have left the church 15 years ago and if you see a former church member in the grocery store what do you do? You hug and greet one another and inquire about the rest of the family as you would seeing a long lost brother. You still feel that connection of the covenant relationship and your heart still wants to know what's going on with the rest of the family.

If your family looks like the first family established by God, meaning, there is a husband, wife and children it doesn't mean you don't have to work at it. Quite the contrary, this is the family units that the enemy is after. The enemy has a great attack against the "first family" figure. Meaning if the enemy can get us off track and away from the relationships God ordained, he has a good chance of destroying all other family units. The reason our society is trying so hard to establish "alternative" family lifestyles is not because they seek to enjoy what God designed for marriage, but rather because the enemy has begun trying to alter and ultimately destroy the family unit that God originally designed and if we are not careful there won't be a family unit at all. We will be a group of people living on the earth each out for his or her own self. We will have lost the very thing God intended – relationship.

So how do we keep our family unit in tact? How do we make sure we are honoring God's covenant relationships?

Let's take steps to ensure that you have a kingdom family – a family that's even better than the Huxtables!

Understanding the Covenant Relationship

Let's begin with the way God intended a family to look like. The bible says God created Adam and then he gave him a gift called Eve. He made Eve from the very flesh of Adam and he joined them together in marriage to be together until death separated them. God's command to Adam and his bride was to be fruitful. They were commanded to populate the earth. They were commanded to bear the fruit of marriage. Basically God instructed Adam and Eve to have children.

When a husband and wife have children their whole world changes. Bill Withers sings a song called *Just The Two of Us* and the lyrics say:

Just the two of us
We can make it if we try
Just the two of us
Just the two of us
Building castles in the sky
Just the two of us
You and I

THY KINGDOM COME

Isn't that a beautiful thought? But once you have children inside a marriage it goes from being just the two of us to being all of us. And believe me when I tell you, one kid can seem like a whole bunch of us! You go from romantic dinners for two to stolen moments in the back closet. You used to unplug the phone so you wouldn't be disturbed from the evening. Now you listen carefully to the baby monitor just praying that baby will sleep through the night. And it doesn't stop there. Just as soon as you're done with listening to baby monitors you find yourself carrying around baby strollers and car seats. And if that's not enough, later you and your husband are having arguments over what age your daughter gets to wear makeup or how late your son should be allowed to hang out after the football game. You go from romantic walks on the beach to chaperoning dances and teenage dates.

There will be more than a time or two when you wonder, "What happened to us?"

You'll long for the days when you were "cool". You'll forget how beautiful your wife's eyes are and from time to time you will not even remember if they are brown or green. But you will remember to make 4 dozen cookies for the PTA bake sale and you will remember to pick up Junior after his soccer game.

Sometimes parenting is a rollercoaster and you will find yourself longing for the times when it was "Just the two of us". Even Cliff and Clair Huxtable had thoughts of, "Maybe we should just give them the house."

Then one day your friend will tell you he and his wife are expecting a baby and you will pat him on the back and genuinely shake his hand and offer him a big congratulations. Your best girlfriend will tell you she's finally pregnant and you will happily shed tears of joy with her and be the first to offer to host her baby shower.

Because all of the above items I just described are the best years of your life. There is nothing you enjoy more than the times with your family. You love coming home every evening to spend time with your beautiful wife and adoring children. You tell stories all day long about your husband and your children to anyone who will listen. Why? Because you have a kingdom family.

You have a covenant connection to other people. It goes from you and your parents to you having the responsibility of your own family. You assume a leadership role instead of simply apart of a team. And no matter what happens to that family unit you must always respect the covenant that brought you together.

Be Fruitful and Multiply!

Isn't it funny that Doctor and Mrs. Huxtable were never tired? We saw countless episodes where they went to work and came home with a smile on their faces. They always had time to gather together around the dinner table and they always had time to listen to the details of their children's day. They never argued about bills or appointments. And not one episode do we see them fighting about money.

How is that possible? What am I missing in my family?

Let a Kingdom Father explain it to you:

I am a kingdom husband and father. My name is not important. The only name that is important is the name of my savior, Jesus Christ. Jesus came that I might have life and have it more abundantly. I live an abundant life and I am a Kingdom Man. Before I married my wife I committed to understanding exactly who I am. I see men all around me looking to their wives to define them as men. I know it is not my wife's job to define me. My wife compliments me. She is my helpmeet. She helps me in every area of our life together. God gave me in a wife - the part of me that was missing. In fact, he designed me with a missing element that could only be completed through marriage. She is the one who holds the piece of me that God held out for marriage. Again, this does not mean she defines me. It simply means she is a part of me and I am a part of her.

Long before marriage I actively engaged in self discovery. I sought God to help me discover who I am and who he wants me to be. I know all of my issues, so to speak. I am fully aware of all of my shortcomings. My wife was not fooled into marrying me. Shortly after we began dating I laid all the cards on the table. We both discussed all of the things that make us who we are. We discussed the things we love, the things we fear, the things that produce laughter and happiness. I expressed my past hurts and pains and made sure I listened as she expressed hers as well.

The bible says when a man marries his wife he is to leave his father and mother and cleave to his wife. My first responsibility is to

God. My second is to my family. There is no other order. Everyone else comes after God and my family. Christians debate the word of God when it says a woman must submit to her husband. As a Kingdom husband I fully understand my wife's submission to me. My wife's submission to me is not like my neighbor's wife's submission to him. My wife fits me and his wife fits him. I never compare my wife and our marriage to that of others. I know that God handpicked my wife for me and he also handpicked me for her. Together we are the perfect couple. We are the foundation of our family.

My family honors God above all else. We laugh together. We cry together. We pray together and we love together. I am the priest of my house. My wife loves and respects me. My children hold me in the highest regard. God is pleased with me as a husband and a father.

That beloved, is a kingdom husband and father. Although I am a woman I write this from the standpoint of a man. Not because I claim to know the mind-set of a man, but because I know many, many kingdom husbands and fathers. In fact, I was raised by one and I am married to one!

As we dig into the kingdom family let's set some goals for the family. There are three key goals for a kingdom family. I like to refer to them as SAW!

- **S**ubmission
- **A**ttention
- **W**orship

A lot has been discussed as it relates to the subject of submission. The Message version of the bible in Ephesians 5:21-28 says:

Out of respect for Christ, be courteously reverent to one another. Wives, understand and support your husbands in ways that show your support for Christ. The husband provides leadership to his wife the way Christ does to his church, not by domineering but by cherishing. So just as the church submits to Christ as he exercises such leadership, wives should likewise submit to their husbands. Husbands, go all out in your love for your wives, exactly as Christ did for the church—a love marked by giving, not getting. Christ's love makes the church whole. His words evoke her beauty. Everything he does and says is designed to bring the best out of her, dressing her in dazzling white silk, radiant with holiness. And that is how husbands ought to love their wives. They're really doing themselves a favor—since they're already "one" in marriage.

Let's look clearly at the goal of submission and find out how to submit ourselves to Christ and His goal for the Kingdom Family.

Ephesians chapter 5, verse 22 says wives are to understand and support your husbands in ways that show your support for Christ. The husband provides leadership to his wife in the way that Christ provides leadership to the church.

Ladies, do you understand your husband? Do you understand the call that God has placed on his life? Do you understand and support his role as the priest of your household? Christ provides leadership to the church. Do you understand and support your husband's leadership in your house?

Christ died for the church. Your kingdom husband would lay down his life for you. And all you have to do is understand and support him. Your husband provides leadership to your family in the way that Christ provides leadership to the church. Now, Christ does not domineer over the church. Christ loves the church. He cherishes the church. Even when Christ doesn't give Christ exactly what he wants, it is always clear that he loves us and wants what is best for us. Likewise, wives should submit to their husbands and husbands should care for their wives.

Men, Ephesians 5:25 begins by saying, husbands, go all out in your love for your wives, exactly as Christ did for the church. There is nothing a Kingdom Husband won't do for his family. He'll move the earth if he has to. Go all out for your wife. Cherish her, love her. This is what Christ did for the church. And this love is marked by giving not getting. As the priest of your house with a wife who submits to you, your job is to give! Your focus should not be on getting, but rather giving! I know that sounds harsh in today's society but the reality is if you give as Christ gave, you will have no problem getting everything your heart desires.

The bible says Christ's love makes the church whole. His words evoke her beauty. Everything he does and says is designed to bring the best out in her. This is how a kingdom husband loves his wife. He speaks kindly and lovingly to her at all times. Even when he is angry she knows he loves her because he doesn't let his anger outweigh his love. Everything he does is designed to bring out the best in his wife.

Men of God you must ask yourself, how am I treating my wife? Do I treat my wife the way Christ treats the church? Am I going all out in my love for her? Do I always speak loving and kind words to her? Is God pleased with me as a husband?

Now that we've established submission let's look more closely at different kingdom family scenarios:

I am Nathan Jones. I am the priest of my house. My wife works inside our home. She is considered the manager of our corporation, "Jones Incorporated". My wife manages everything in our home from breakfast to goodnight dreams. She ensures that our home is clean, our meals are cooked and our children are well taken care of. She tends to our every need. My wife manages our family finances. She ensures that all bills are paid in full and on time. She is our chief financial officer. She is also our vacation planner, appointment maker, nurse, and coach. She is my biggest cheerleader. I work outside the home and I often work long hours. My wife plans family events around my schedule so that I can have time with our children. My wife and I also have time alone together. I work hard for my family and together we enjoy a good life. God has blessed us and every night before bed, we thank Him for His goodness.

My name is Kathy Carter. I am the wife and mother of 4 children. I work outside the home. My husband also works. We both have college degrees and work at professions we love. God is the head of our family and my husband is God's right hand man. God speaks to my husband as the priest of our family and my husband is the leader of our family. Our home is paid for from the financial support of both our incomes. We have a bank account that we each contribute to monthly that supports our household bills and other financial obligations. We each also have separate savings accounts that we use to plan special events and vacations for each other and the family. We have no secrets in our family and my husband and I share everything. Our children are happy, health and, well educated children. They honor us by understanding and honoring their role in the family. Our children understand their role is to put God first and then our family. Our children clearly understand our views on education, dating, drugs, etc. and they obey us knowing that we have their best interest at heart. Our family worships together in prayer and bible study and we also attend church together happily and joyfully as a family.

My name is Tijuana Winters. I am a single mother of two children. Each of my children has a different father. The boundaries of my family stretch to include each of my children's fathers although I am not married to either of them. The reason is because through our children God has called for us to maintain a covenant relationship. Because of our children together we are a family. I never disrespect my child's father and I never speak negatively about him. We work together to create a loving family for our child. I pray for the father of my child every day. God is the head of my family and he gives me direction and instruction on how to run my household and raise my children on a daily basis. I look to God daily for his love and support. I train my children to seek God first in everything they do. My family attends church regularly, for this is our support system and also our family.

My name is Tyrone Douglas and I am the father of four children. I have three children with my current wife and one child with my ex-wife. I am the priest of my household but I am also in a covenant relationship with my ex-wife because we share the blessing of a child. My child that lives outside of my home always has a place inside my home with my wife and other children. There is no difference between my children. I love and care for them all equally. My wife understands that my ex-wife is apart of our family. She is not threatened, intimidated or insecure about my ex-wife because she knows that I am totally committed to her and our life together. My wife and my ex-wife respect each other and often talk about things that relate to our children. God is the source for my family and His word is my instruction manual.

Can you find yourself in either of these statements? Is this how you speak about your family? If you do not find yourself in either of these scenarios and you are struggling to submit to your family in a way that pleases God, please know that God is able to help you. God wants you to have healthy, loving relationships with your family. God created us to be relational. The root of the word relationship is relate. God created us to be able to relate or to share consistently with one another in love and harmony. If your family life needs, help keep reading. The next key point is attention.

THY KINGDOM COME

Where Attention Goes…

In the military the word attention usually follows with a salute or an acknowledgement to a fellow officer or superior. As a superior officer approaches, a soldier, or group of individuals is called to Attention by the first person noticing the officer. The officer or group salutes the approaching officer with a raised hand to the head motion. In old military movies a group leader would often shout, "Attention!" This is a sign of respect. When you give attention to your family this is a sign of respect to God. You respect God enough to pay attention and give time to the covenant He has established.

Anything you don't feed eventually dies. Many people are literally starving their families to death by not giving them attention. We see articles in the news that families are breaking up. The world calls it "irreconcilable differences". I call it starvation! We are literally starving our families.

As it relates to your family, you must give attention or acknowledgement in two ways. One, you must give attention to your God. Salute him and give him attention and acknowledgement. You must also salute and give attention and acknowledgement to your family.

The bible says in Proverbs 3:6 - *In all thy ways acknowledge him and he will direct your paths*. Family is a path. It's a journey that requires God's direction. Once you direct your attention to God, and do what pleases him in your family, he will direct everything else.

THY KINGDOM COME

God created us to have relationships. God created the family. Then why is it that we oftentimes leave him out of them. We go to church week after week and we jump and shout but then we come home and fail in our families. It's because we fail to acknowledge Him in our family. Give attention to God in your family. Seek him concerning your family. Pray for your family daily. And once you pray, know that it's already done. God has already answered your prayers. If you have asked God to repair your family relationships, he's already done it the minute you prayed. If you have asked God to repair your relationship with the mother of your children or your ex-husband, God heard you and he has already blessed and given you what you have asked for.

But do you believe it enough to receive it? The bible teaches us to call those things that be not as though they already were. (Romans 4:17) Your ex-husband doesn't need to change, you do. You need to call what you believe. Stop calling what you see, and start speaking to what you believe God has done. You speak kind words. You say please and thank you. You invite your ex-wife on a family outing with the rest of your family. Begin to believe God by acting "as if".

Give attention to the thing you have prayed for. If you prayed for more time with your family, look for ways to have more time with your family. If you prayed for the mother of your child to be kinder, act as if she is. Speak more kindly towards her. Do something nice for her. Help her begin to act differently.

Give attention to your family and family situations. Where God's attention goes, God's love flows! Give attention to God and he will cause love to flow in every area you bring to His attention.

Let Us Worship Christ

The last and final key point is worship.

Romans Chapter 12 verses 1-2 from the King James Version of the bible says:

I beseech you therefore, brethren, by the mercies of God, that ye present your bodies a living sacrifice, holy, acceptable unto God, which is your reasonable service.
And be not conformed to this world: but be ye transformed by the renewing of your mind, that ye may prove what is that good, and acceptable, and perfect, will of God.

Give God everything you've got. It is your reasonable service. This same passage of scripture in the Message Version of the Bible says:

So here's what I want you to do, God helping you: Take your everyday, ordinary life—your sleeping, eating, going-to-work, and walking-around life—and place it before God as an offering. Embracing what God does for you is the best thing you can do for him. Don't become so well-adjusted to your culture that you fit into it without even thinking. Instead, fix your attention on God. You'll be changed from the inside out. Readily recognize what he wants from you, and quickly respond to it. Unlike the culture around you, always dragging you down to its level of immaturity, God brings the best out of you, develops well-formed maturity in you.

Offer God your family. Offer God everything you have. Place your family before God as an offering. This is the best thing you can do for your family. This is actually worship. When we define worship we have to understand the English word, "worship" actually comes from two words: weorth, which means "worth" and ship which means "quality". This means worth quality. If something is worth quality it means it should be revered, respected, honored. God is definitely worth quality. He is worthy. Worship means to declare God's worth. In biblical terms, when we praise God, we are declaring his worth. As it relates to the family, when we do the right things within our families, we are again declaring God's worth. 1 Peter 2:9 teaches us that we were called for the purpose of praising and worshipping God. By establishing Kingdom Families we are declaring God's worth to the world. God created Adam, gave him Eve and commanded that they establish a family. It's God's will that we have Kingdom Families.

Family is a ministry. No matter who you are and what you are called to do, family is also part of your personal ministry. No one escapes family. Everyone has one. Everyone is born into a family and everyone is given a family by God. Throughout your life your family may change. You may add to it through marriage, birth, and also by church. It is your reasonable service to worship God through your family relationships. Your family is designed to worship God.

It honors God when you have healthy relationships within your family. It proves he is God. It proves that God is alive and still at work. There's an old wives tale that says, "The family that prays together…stays together." Now I've known a lot of old wives and more often than not, they are right about everything!

When was the last time your family worshipped together? I don't mean, when was the last time you went to church; I mean, when was the last time you worshipped together? A lot of families to go to the same church but they don't necessarily worship together. How about getting up on Sunday morning and setting the atmosphere for worship. Turn on the good, Christian music while you're getting dressed. Talk about church. Get excited about church together. Talk about church on the way to church. Build anticipation about church. Then when you get there, sit together and enjoy yourself. Have a ball in Jesus as a family. Then when you get back in the car, talk about what happened at church. Build excitement around your worship. Talk about the message. Ask the children what they learned. Tell them what you learned. Spend time worshipping together. And not just on Sunday. Begin a family bible study. Pick a day of the week and spend 30 minutes together playing bible bingo or reading scripture and discussing it. Make it fun and interesting for the kids. Talk about what the bible says about certain things in their lives. What better way to worship God!

When was the last time your family thanked God for his blessings in your family? Psalm 100 from the Message version of the Bible says this:

A Thanksgiving Psalm

On your feet now—applaud God! Bring a gift of laughter, sing yourselves into his presence. Know this: God is God, and God, God. He made us; we didn't make him. We're his people, his well-tended sheep. Enter with the password: "Thank you!" Make yourselves at home, talking praise. Thank him. Worship him. For God is sheer beauty, all-generous in love, loyal always and ever!

Finally, it doesn't matter at all what your family looks like. Some families have 12 people and some families have 2. It's still family. Honor God by loving and having healthy relationships with the people he has put in your life. Remember, it's a blood covenant. God shed his blood for your family. He has bound you together with people and it's your job to take care of that relationship. It's your job to nurture it. This pleases God and it's your reasonable service to live a life filled with love, peace and joy. You deserve the best in life…anything less is an insult to God!

Kingdom Children
Ambassador Wilson

Teach your children to choose the right path, and when they are older, they will remain upon it. (Proverbs 22:6 - NLT)

In the book of Proverbs chapter 22 begins by discussing a good name or good reputation. In verse 2 it tells us that a rich man and a poor man were both made by God, because truly all are made by God. But what is it that separates a rich man and a poor man? What separates a happy man from a miserable man? What is the difference between a man with a good reputation and a man with a bad reputation? What separates the two? The only thing that separates the two is the choices they have made in life! Your life is defined by a series of choices you have made to date. And what about your children?

As part of making choices for your own life, you also have to make good choices for your children. In chapter 22 of Proverbs it begins by instructing us to choose a good reputation over great riches. But then in verse six, there is nestled a great hidden treasure:

Point your kids in the right direction—
when they're old they won't be lost.
(Proverbs 22:6 – The Message)

What do we want for our children? Do we even know anymore?

THY KINGDOM COME

Let me begin by saying your children should become greater than you! There lives should turn out better than your life.

Why? Because they have you as a mentor and teacher. You are there to teach your children. You are there to train your children. They have the benefit of learning from your mistakes and not having to make the same mistakes you made. They have the benefit of your intercessory prayers. They have the benefit of your experience – the joys and the pains.

The society we live in today teaches our children to give in to the things of their flesh. Society also instructs our children to do what feels good. Our children are taught at an early age to seek after material things. The more stuff you have the better you are. Children are often instructed to do what everyone else is doing.

But the bible doesn't instruct us to allow the world to teach our children in the way they should go. The bible instructs us…the Christian parents…to teach our children.

Our clear instruction is to train up Kingdom Children. So what does a Kingdom Child look like?

Let's take a look together. Let's go into the mind of a Kingdom Kid:

"Superheroes often live very normal lives. That is until one day they begin to discover their purpose and their hidden abilities. That is the case with Kingdom Children. I am much like a super-

hero. I have hidden talents and abilities that God has placed down on the inside of me. My parents are Ambassadors for Jesus Christ and part of their purpose is to assist me in unlocking those hidden talents and abilities.

Once I began to discover my purpose in the earth I became unstoppable. I know who I am. I know who I belong to and how I am expected to behave. No secular music influences me. No satanic television shows clog my mind; for I am an ambassador. I am a Kingdom Kid. The kingdom of heaven resides in me.

I may be a teenager, or I could be an even younger kid no more than 7 years old. It doesn't matter because I live a kingdom life. I live life as an ambassador for those my age. My actions are an example to the world of the Christ that lives in me.

How did I get this way you may ask. Well, it started with the word of God. My parents taught me the word of God and from the moment I began learning the word of God, my powers began to surface. I began to have supernatural abilities beyond that of my peers.

My parents taught me simple prayers. Each day I begin and end my day in prayer. I spend time talking to God even though I am a child. Each day I pray and ask God to give me direction for the day. I pray for my school and my teachers. I pray for the children who attend my school. I also pray every day that God would open my mind so that I may learn. At the end of the day I thank God for a great day. I pray for my family, my friends and all the people of the world. I pray that people everywhere will begin to understand the kingdom principles and live the way God wants us to live.

Each school day I give my focus to my teachers who are the authority that God has placed over my life for the school day. I am obedient to my teachers for I know God has placed them in my life to teach me. I can be obedient to my teachers even if they are not kingdom believers because God is still in control of them as it relates to me. I have favor with my teachers and my Principal. They know who I am and they work to assist me in being an excellent student.

I have several faith confessions that I speak over my own life. I understand that life is in the power of my tongue, therefore I constantly speak life in my own life and in the lives of others. No corrupt communication comes from my mouth.

I have note cards that I keep in a box near my bed. Written on these note cards are my faith confessions and my personal affirmations. Sometimes I take a card or two with me to school. It reminds me of who I am and what I want to accomplish.

Here are two of my favorite faith confessions:

> *"I am an Ambassador for the Kingdom of Heaven. God has given me supernatural ability for learning. I can learn and comprehend anything because God is in me. In Jesus' Name, Amen."*

THY KINGDOM COME

"I am an Ambassador for Christ. I walk like, talk like and act like Christ. I have favor with God and with people. I live as God wants me to live. In Jesus' Name, Amen."

Here are a few of my affirmation quotes:

"I am smart."
"I am beautiful."
"I can learn anything."
"I am obedient."
"I enjoy math and science."
"I speak good things."
"I have great friends."
"I am a great friend."

My parents never have to worry about me falling in with a bad crowd. My close friends are ambassadors as well. My parents know the parents of all my friends. I do know some people who are not quite ambassadors yet. But in these relationships I know my purpose is to help them become ambassadors. I am not influenced by these people; I am set to influence them. I have clear boundaries set by my parents as it relates to who I can spend time with. I also have clear boundaries set by my parents as it relates to where I can and cannot go. I understand there are some places that are not appropriate for someone of my stature. I am not concerned with what people say or think about me. I am more concerned with what my parents and God think about me.

I know there are a lot of parents in the "world" who are worried about children and sex. My parents do not worry about me having premarital sex. I am an ambassador. And an ambassador does not engage in premarital sex. My parents have helped me to understand that sex was created by God and it was designed to be enjoyed by a husband and a wife when they are married. I understand that having sex before marriage goes against God and it can hurt me both physically and emotionally.

When dating, my parents meet every person I wish to date. My parents have sat down with this individual and talked with him/her. My parents have explained to the person I wish to date that I am an ambassador. My parents have explained to him/her that I am special and that I am to be well taken care of. My parents explained to my potential date that in order to date me he/she has to know Christ and attend church. My parents have also explained to my potential suitor that sex before marriage is not an option. Each person who wishes to date me has the opportunity to change his/her mind once the boundaries have been established. My parents outline curfew, dating rules and places that I may attend. My date clearly understands who I am and what it takes to date me.

I know this may sound a bit strange to some of you but it works in a kingdom family. There are some children who think my parents are too strict or try to encourage me to disobey my parents. But I know the benefits to being a Kingdom kid! I also know the consequences of disobedience. As a child, God has placed my parents in authority over my life. God has also given me a sound mind to be able to make good and wise decisions.

As a Kingdom Kid, I have more advantages in life than my peers. I have all the material things the most kids have. My parents provide everything I need and they make sure that I have everything that is good for me. For the bible teaches us that "no good thing will He withhold from us." I have the much of same material things as other kids. I have a cell phone, an Ipod, cable television and the like. I have some designer clothing, tennis shoes, etc. But the material things my parents have provided for me do not define me. I do not hunger after them. I clearly understand that God is the source of everything. The things I have been given are a blessing from God. I do not worship the gift, I have been taught to worship the Giver.

Yes I have boundaries that are put in place to guide me and protect me, but I have something other children do not have. I have peace. I watch other children at my school as they struggle with life. It's odd to me to see young people struggling with so much. They cry because they are hurting over something someone has said to them or done to them. I know their tears are real and the pain they feel is honest and true pain. I listen to them talk about the boy who took their virginity and never called again. I feel sad for them when I hear them talk about going into rehab for crack or alcohol addictions. But these are the things the boundaries in my life have kept me from.

I openly discuss these issues with my parents and together we pray for the youth of this generation.

My parents allow me to attend concerts from time to time. I have attended some great concerts performed by Christian and Gos-

pel artists. I have also attended some great performances of R&B singers and performers. As I sat in the concerts I saw people young and old worshipping. In both the Christian and R&B concerts there was worship. But the thing I noticed was that in the Christian concerts everyone there was worshipping God. And it was a beautiful thing to be apart of. But in the R&B concerts the people were worshipping the singer. Now don't get me wrong, I truly appreciate the gift that God has given the singer, but I could not understand how people can give worship to a gift.

I have also heard some rap music. When I was younger my parents would sit down with me and listen with me. Together we would discuss the lyrics. My parents would explain to me what the lyrics meant. Sometimes we would get out the dictionary and together we would go through the words to get clear definitions. After a while I didn't want to listen to most rap music anymore. Something about it hurts my feelings. I choose not to listen to anything that hurts my feelings. Now don't misunderstand me, there are some songs that I enjoy listening to. There are some artists who use their rap lyrics to inspire and uplift. But I choose who I will listen to and don't feel pressure to run out and buy music just because others are doing it. I listen to what makes me feel good.
I am an Ambassador for the young people of my generation. I thank God that he has blessed me. I thank God for having a protective barrier around me. Do I sound like your kid?"

Do these thoughts sound like your child? If not, please don't be discouraged. It's not too late. As long as the sun rose this morning, God is still God and He is able to turn around any situation.

We know that life is defined by the choices we make. And as a parent, you have to make kingdom choices in order to produce a kingdom child. So now that we've been given a glimpse into the mind of a kingdom kid. How do we as parents train them? How do we unlock the superheroes God has given us charge over?

Raising a Superhero – Raising a Kingdom Kid!

Let's start at the beginning! God has blessed you with a beautiful gift. A bundle of joy!

Please understand that no matter the circumstance in which your baby is born of, it is still a gift from God. Whether you became pregnant out of wedlock or you became pregnant in wedlock but at what you considered the wrong time. Your baby is still a gift from God. You may be pregnant right now and in the middle of a divorce. The baby is still a gift. No baby comes into the world without God's approval. No baby comes into this world without a plan and a purpose designed by God. For the bible declares, *"I knew you before I formed you in your mother's womb. Before you were born I set you apart and appointed you as my prophet to the nations." (Jeremiah 1:5 – NLT)*

It matters not the conditions surrounding the birth of your baby. You may have planned your gift. You may be like me; you may have begged God for the opportunity to become a parent. No matter how your baby entered the world, I want to be the first tell you this:

One false move and you can ruin that kid's life!

Now that I've frightened you, get off the ledge and let's talk it through.

Born into the Kingdom – The Infantry Stage

But Jesus said, Suffer little children, and forbid them not, to come unto me: for of such is the kingdom of heaven.
(Matthew 19:14 – KJV)

Your baby is born. During the first 6 years of that baby's life is what I like to call the infantry stage. From the age of inception through the age of 6 you have three goals:

- Feed
- Nurture
- Protect

These stages are critical. Anything you don't feed will die. It will die of starvation. This is physically and spiritually. You must, of course, physically feed a child or it will die. But if you do not feed the child spiritually, it will also die. The way to feed a child spiritually is through love. If you do not love the child you are, in essence, starving it. And again, anything that is not fed will die. You must also nurture the child. To nurture means to care for, look after, or to cultivate. Every good parent learns to nurture their child. We play classical music so the child might grow up to be intelligent. We read bedtime stories and fairy tales to children before they are even old enough to understand. We rock them in our arms when they are uneasy. In the same manner, we are to spiritually nurture our children. Your child should be taught the word of God in the same way we teach fairy tales. Spiritually you are the link between the child and God. Until the child is old enough to speak to God, it is your job to do the talking for him/her.

To protect the child is also a physical and a spiritual thing. You must physically do everything in your power to protect the child from harm. This of course means making sure nothing will harm the child. When parents are expecting a baby, they set up protective measure by baby proofing their home to make sure no harm comes to the child. Good parents keep harmful and hazardous products out of reach of the child. This is all great. However, you must also spiritually protect your child. You must keep harmful and hazardous things of a spiritual nature away from your child. This is not a deep as it sounds. This simply means you have to pray for your child. During this important stage of life you must pray daily for your child. This also goes back to feeding your child spiritually. Beginning at an early stage, let your child hear you talk about Jesus and the love He has for your baby. Make it part of your "baby talk". One of your child's earliest memories should be you telling him/her about the Savior.

Feeding your child spiritually is just as important as Gerber and Similac feeding formulas. Anytime you invite the Father into a child's life you are honoring God. Even Jesus taught the disciples to bring the children to him. Jesus wants to bless your children.

THY KINGDOM COME

Now that we've defined the infantry stage, let's move on to the next stage.

Kingdom Kid

The Kingdom Kid phase takes place between the ages of 7 – 12.

During this time you have four main goals:

- Speaking Blessings
- Affirmation
- Uncovering Gifts
- Teaching Prayer

You may be thinking to yourself, "I already blew it. I just got this book and my kid is already eight or nine years old." You are not too late. Even if you missed the infant stages you can still grab a hold to these next important concepts. If your child is already in the age range for a kingdom kid, you can begin here at the kingdom kid stage and your child will blossom.

Children are very adaptable. They are nothing like adults. They are not stuck in their ways. They don't easily settle into traditions and habits like adults do. Children will grasp new concepts very easily. They are actually conditioned by God to adapt to change. So if your child is between the ages of seven and twelve, please take these four stages and run with them. Introduce them now and see how your child's life quickly begins to change.

THY KINGDOM COME

The first step in raising a kingdom kid is to begin to speak blessings. In the bible when Jacob was near death the bible says he lined his children in front of him and he spoke blessings into their lives. *(Genesis 49:1-28)*

What you say to your child is far more important than what the world says to him/her.

By the age of seven you must begin to speak blessings into your child's life on a daily basis. You must speak what you want for your child's life. Let your child know that you believe he/she is the best. Praise your child's abilities and talents.

"You are smart. You are talented. You are gifted. You are an excellent student. You are beautiful. You are handsome. You can do it. You are blessed. You are healthy. You are wealthy. You are strong. You are loved."

Then take it a step further. Everyday affirm your child. If your child can read, write affirmations down on index cards and every day spend some time reading the affirmations with your child. Let your child know that you are proud of him/her. Oftentimes as parents we are quick to tell our children when they mess up. But how often do we affirm them? Your praise should outweigh your corrective actions.

When I was a young girl probably about 12 years old I was in the locker room of my junior high school after gym class and a fellow classmate walked over to me and looked me square in the eye and said, "You're black and you're ugly." I was in shock. I stood there for a moment in complete shock. I dressed and resumed my day. When I got home I looked in the mirror at my face and what looked back at me was the same girl I'd always seen. I starred in the mirror for a moment and shrugged it off. "She must be crazy," I thought. "I'm beautiful." I went on about my day and never gave thought to the girl's words again. In fact, I saw her everyday and she never uttered those words again.

"What happened?" You may ask. I heard what the girl said but it did not register in my mind because it contradicted what I had been taught about myself. It went against what my parents and those who loved me proclaimed in my life. I was a very dark complexioned little girl. In fact I was darker than both my parents. But my parents knew the secret of affirmation. Over and over again my parents affirmed to me that I was pretty. I was special. They affirmed that my dark skin was beautiful. Constantly I was told I was a "pretty black girl". This let me know that while my skin color was darker than some, I was also still pretty.

Looking back I was an average looking girl. I looked pretty much like every other African American girl in my neighborhood. But also looking back I remember always being complimented. Adults were always complimenting me. Adults often told me that I was pretty. "What a pretty girl you are," they'd say. "Look at your beautiful complexion."

What made me a pretty girl wasn't my outer appearance. What made me a pretty girl were the affirmations that were placed inside of me. These affirmations made me walk taller. They made me smile my brightest smile. These affirmations made me use my gifts and talents with confidence. These affirmations made me walk with a glow that told the world that I was special and I was loved.

During the ages of seven to twelve it is also a parent's job to begin uncovering the gifts and talents that God has placed in a child. God has a plan and a purpose for your child. It is your job to begin to help your child slowly discover God's plan and purpose for their life. Every child is blessed with unique talents and gifts. Unique talents and gifts are the things your child does easily and almost effortlessly. As early as possible being trying to discover what things your child does well. Is your child gifted at piano? Is your child gifted at singing? Does mathematics come easily? Does your child have the gift of gab? Does your child have a great memory?

Encourage those gifts and talents. Encourage your child to use them daily and grow in them. Buy books and games for your child to help him/her grow in these gifts and talents. It may be one gift that you discover quickly or it may be several gifts that develop over time. It is your job to help your child discover his/her gifts and talents. Sometimes it takes years of lessons of all kinds. You may try tennis lessons, ballet lessons, tuba lessons, etc. Keep trying. Keep developing.

Now this does not mean you should forget about the things your child is not naturally gifted in doing. Not at all. Just because your child is not naturally gifted at English doesn't mean you should ignore his/her English grades. This means you should use the other gifts and talents to help him/her with the English grade. Just because English is a challenge doesn't mean it should be ignored.

Quite the contrary. English is a challenge and you should work harder with your child to show him/her that he/she can do it. For the bible says “I can do all things through Christ which strengthens me.”

As you begin uncovering gifts and talents teach your child to push. Push harder to become even more gifted. If your child is gifted at singing, push him/her to take up an instrument. Push your child to spend time developing those musical gifts. If your child has the gift of gab, encourage him/her to speak publicly. Encourage him/her to write poetry or stories and enter them into writing contests.

The last goal for a Kingdom Kid is to teach prayer. Every morning and every evening teach your child to pray. At this age begin teaching your child the Ask, Believe, Receive concept.

Teach your child to ask for the things he/she desires. Then teach them to believe they shall have them. This also reverts back into the affirmations. Teach your child ask God and then write down the thing he is believing God for, in the present tense. “I am a straight A student, in Jesus’ Name.” That is the believe factor. The more they believe it, the more they receive it.

Teach your child to also pray for the needs of the family and others. Between the ages of seven and twelve develop your child’s prayer life. Have him/her lead the family in prayer a few times a week. Teach your child to pray for teachers, friends, and also enemies. Teach him/her to pray for their grades.

The Superhero

The last stage of developing a superhero is called, Superhero. The superhero stage falls between the ages of thirteen and eighteen.

You have four objectives at this stage:

- Exercising Super Powers
- Self Preservation
- Prayer Warrior
- Shifting into a Kingdom Man/Woman

Between the ages of thirteen and eighteen years of age your child is aware of his/her gifts, talents and "super powers". Your job is to first begin teaching your child to exercise those super powers.

We are all born with natural gifts and talents. Those talents can be used for good or they can be used for evil. Your child might have the gift of gab. Now is the time to begin teaching your child to exercise that superpower for good. Encourage your child to speak good words and not negative words. Encourage your child to speak at school assemblies or church functions. Possibly enroll your child in a drama club or start a new one in your neighborhood.

Your child may have an extraordinary gift of dance. The bible teaches us that every gift we have should be used to worship and praise God. Even dance was given by God for His use. If your child is gifted in dance, encourage it. Encourage him/her to use the gift in praise and worship dancing. Encourage him/her to dance in different Christian based dance theaters or you might even encourage your child to start his/her own dance troop.

Whatever gift your child inhabits it is your job to encourage its use. And always give great praise when your child is exercising their gifts and talents.

The more your child uses these gifts and talents the more super they become – hence, superpowers!

The second phase of a super hero is Self Preservation.

At this stage your child becomes aware of the power of choice. At this age your child becomes very aware of his/her mortality. It is your job to encourage your child to make wise choices and good decisions. When you see someone on television or on the news that has made a bad decision, talk it over with your child. Ask questions like, "Why do you think he made that decisions? What do you think will happen if you make that choice? What should have been done differently?"

Encourage dialog with your child to get him/her thinking about the power of their choices. Make sure you child understands that one bad choice can change their life.

This is a critical stage to encourage honesty. At this stage your child begins to understand the power of disappointment. No child wants to disappoint their parents. Please instill in your child that they can always talk to you and you will listen and help. Speak openly and honestly with your children about your life and the choices you made when you were their age. This is the stage where you really begin to mentor your child. The word mentor means a wise and trusted counselor. A great mentor is someone who allows you to see into themselves. You get to see their successes as well as their failures. Spend quality time talking openly and honestly with your child. The key thing to remember is that your child is destined for greatness and it is your ministry to help prepare them. Give to them freely, the benefit of your life.

A Superhero Lives Here!

So here's what I want you to do, God helping you: Take your everyday, ordinary life—your sleeping, eating, going-to-work, and walking-around life—and place it before God as an offering. Embracing what God does for you is the best thing you can do for him. Don't become so well-adjusted to your culture that you fit into it without even thinking. Instead, fix your attention on God. You'll be changed from the inside out. Readily recognize what he wants from you, and quickly respond to it. Unlike the culture around you, always dragging you down to its level of immaturity, God brings the best out of you, develops well-formed maturity in you. (Romans 12:1-2 The Message)

You have spent years teaching your child kingdom principles. The one thing you have consistently taught is prayer. At this stage your child becomes a prayer warrior.

Encourage your child to spend quality time with God asking but also listening. Encourage him/her to give everything to God. Your child should understand clearly the power of prayer. Your child now prays with you in a family setting of prayer. If you are sick, your child has been trained to lay hands on you and go to God in prayer for your health. Your only job here is to keep talking to your child about the goodness of God and pray with him/her.

The final stage of a super hero is the stage where your child shifts into a Kingdom Man or Kingdom Woman.

As your child matures and reaches the ages of 17 or 18 they begin to make the shift into adulthood.

By this age your child is not a child anymore but beginning to walk in authority as an ambassador. You see the fruits of your labor so to speak. You have helped God raise up a kingdom man or woman and it shows.

Your son/daughter is making great choices. Your son/daughter speaks with authority. You have done your job well and God is pleased.

Please understand that everyone makes mistakes. It's part of the learning process. But the bible assures *that God causes everything to work together for the good of those who love God and are called according to his purpose. (Romans 8:28 – NLT)* Even the mistakes will work out for good. Because you have trained your child to love the Lord, your child clearly understands that he/she has a purpose and they are fully committed to walking in that purpose.

All thanks and praises to God…you have raised a superhero and he/she will take authority over the earth!

Kingdom Singles Ambassador Walls

An Ambassador Living the Singles Life

I discovered a map one day that was put together by the National Geographic Magazine (February 2007). This map showed a large majority of the single men in the U.S. lived on the west coast while the majority of single women lived on the east coast. The Mississippi river seemed to be the dividing line. There were 40,000 more single men than women in the Los Angles, Long Beach and Santa Ana, CA area and there were 185,000 more single women than men in New York, Newark, New Jersey, and Connecticut.

This map caused me to believe men and women are often separated by the places we live or the environment we live. It also showed me society has made it easy to live a "single life". There are countless opportunities to remain single and independent for both men and women.

The vision of the white picket fence, little dog, children and the mate of our dreams somehow seems to be rapidly fading away. It used to be that the majority of the TV shows centered on family. Don't you remember those classics like Dick Van Dyke, Leave it to Beaver, The Partridge Family, The Brady Bunch, Good Times, I Love Lucy, The Honeymooners, and The Jefferson's, just to name a few. All those classic TV shows illustrated families. We watched families in their good seasons and in their bad seasons. Notice now our TV shows today are often centered around being single and single-parented homes. What happened? In my personal opinion it seems we have a misconstrued conception of INDEPENDENCE. The feeling "I can do this all by myself and I don't need anybody else," has taken over and overshadowed the family structure we use to live by. God created male and female and he joined them together to have rule and dominion in covenant with Him. So why now do we feel we can do it all by ourselves? It is this society of independence and a free world that has given us the illusion that we don't need each other and independence is the way to go. In independence there are no hassles and no commitments…it's just me. I can do whatever I want, whenever I want, with whomever I want.

Now, it may sound to you that I am not supporting singleness. This is definitely not true. I believe singleness to be the most important stage of a person's life; it is a time of discovery, a time of conditioning and a time of preparation. But there is a difference between Earthly Singles and Kingdom Singles, let's take a look:

Who Are You Living For?

Are you an Earthly Single, living a life with a "you" agenda? Everything you do today will be for the satisfaction of yourself. Your achievements are noted because you are educated, skillful and nobody can do it better than you. In fact, your whole day is centered on letting everybody know how great you are and without you in the office everything would fall too pieces. No praises are given to God. Maybe you don't even know who God is, or maybe you don't even think He exists. Why would you thank Him for all the hard work you have done all by yourself? Perhaps you go to church every Sunday, serve on any and every possible committee but you still have a "you" agenda. You are the one who does what you do even in the church. It's all about you. You strive for recognition and appreciation. It's all about you. Is this your life?

Or are you a Kingdom Single? You wake up every morning with God on your mind. As a Kingdom Single praise and worship is pouring from your mouth and protruding from your lips even before your feet even hit the floor. You don't worry about being too loud, it's just you and God and he loves it when you praise him. You begin your day with your God, seeking his direction and attention for the day ahead. All throughout the day you thank and praise God. You thank him for every job well done. You praise him for giving you gifts and talents. You are God's man. You are God's woman.

Which Relationship Is Your Priority?

Are you the Earthly Single and your priorities focus on trying to please people or even yourself? Living a life doing whatever it takes to move up the corporate ladder even when it goes against your personal morals and values. Earthly Singles, are you seeking approval from the person who is supposed to love you? Are you putting others first in an effort to please them or in order to feel loved? Something or someone in your life has become your idol and now you worship it. Your priority is your career, your education? Could your priority be the man you hope will one day marry you? Or could your priority be that beautiful woman who you are trying desperately to win her heart? What, instead of God, earthly single is your priority in life?

A Kingdom Single makes God first priority in their lives. They desire to get closer to God in relationship in order to discover who they really are. Each day your "fellowship" moves deeper and deeper toward "relationship" with God. Every day you hear clearly from your Divine creator the directions you should take on this singleness journey. You are living for and only trying to please God.

Where Is Your Faith?

As an Earthly Single does your beliefs heavily rely on your capabilities, how much you have obtained through education and the experiences of life? You have a mentality of a "dog eat, dog world". Only in tough times or by accident do you find yourself thinking of God hoping that it's not too late to get your life right this time. Then you turn back to your old ways when things are going well and you completely forget about the God who helped you. That is, until something bad happens again. You have faith in the world and the people of the world. That is who you call upon first.

Or are you the Kingdom Single who knows your strength, security, joy and peace come from God who created you to have dominion. As a Kingdom Single you know your faith can withstand any situation and circumstance. You are a conqueror through Christ.

Each day you uphold the creed to "walk by faith, and not by sight" knowing that what the world presents to you is just an "illusion". Your faith calls you to see through the "eyes of God". You constantly seek His truth because of this, you able to maximize on all the blessings God has personally ordained for your life.

Which are you? Are you an earthly single or a Kingdom Single? Or, are you somewhere in between? Don't fret, it is not too late. If you find yourself leaning a little towards an earthly single, there is good news for you. It's time to get focused!

How to Get Focused and Walk as a Kingdom Single

- Have clear vision and stay focused on how good God is, and give thanks daily.

- Remain focused on the all of the things God has provided for you and never be concerned about the things you don't have. God supplies all of your needs. If you don't have it, you don't need it right now!

- Focus on your relationship with God and the purpose He has for your life. Let your prayers be about your submission to Him and the acceptance of His will for your life. Learn to be con tent in your current state.

- Make your desires known to God and speak them from your mouth but don't become obsessed with getting a mate. Seek ye first the kingdom of God and all the other things will be given to you.

- Get busy! Continue to sow good seed in the kingdom of God. There is no time for loneliness and self-pity when you are busy doing God's will. Don't be idle but become active. Get active in your church, in your community, on your job. Remember, you are an Ambassador for Christ. It's your job to change the atmosphere causing positive influences…you can't do this sitting at home alone.

- Stick with it. Many times it appears as if married couples dominate the church. It may seem as if your church does not cater to your needs as a single. Seek ways to introduce new ministries for singles to the church. Integrate activities that support Kingdom Singles. Lift up Christ in your activities and He will draw the people.

- Seek God in your relationships. You are an ambassador. It is natural for people to be attracted to you. However, know that everyone who is attracted to you is not a potential mate. Seek God's directions for all relationships.

- Honor your friendships. A great friend is hard to find and even harder to keep. God has blessed you with great friendships. Honor those friendships. Do everything you can to cultivate them.

Do I Really Want to Say "I Do" - A Singles Dilemma

As a single there are benefits we do enjoy but have you been faced with the decision to say "I do"? So many questions may run through our mind as we face this challenge of making a lifelong commitment. And will this "I Do" take away all the wonderful benefits of the single life?

If we are honest with ourselves we are a bit reserved and uncertain as to whether we want the "I do" or continue our journey living the single life. Even others make it a bit difficult to make the right decisions because of their own personal opinions, you've heard them before…you're getting kind of old aren't you?...the longer you wait, the harder it will be have children, and the best one of them all don't wait to late and be an old maid". You should never feel pressured into marriage just keep your sights on God, enjoy life as a Kingdom single and he will give you the desires of your heart.

And If your desire is to one day say "I Do" keep focused on God to avoid entering into that covenant relationship that turns out to be not so covenant. An old adage Mama use to say, "All shine isn't gold, and what looks good to you isn't always good for you." If your relationship is based on looks this not a good measurement toward securing a stable marriage.

I've heard Ambassador Wade state in the past that she wants the single life, and also she wants the married life too. What a great dilemma of wanting both worlds without sacrificing the benefits of both. My answer for you is to relax and let go because God has it all in control where you will never have to give up but you will only increase in His glorious blessings. Enjoy the fruit of your singleness and all that God has provided for you.

THY KINGDOM COME

While You're Waiting

If a mate is what you desire, get yourself ready. The bible says a man who finds a wife finds a good thing. What will he find when he comes your way? While you are waiting for that husband, while you are waiting for that wife, what are you doing?

If you are a single woman and your desire is to be a Kingdom Wife, make sure that when he finds you, he finds a wife. Get your life in order. When the bible describes a virtuous woman what did she have? She had her stuff together didn't she? She had property, money, and businesses. What will a man find when he comes your way? Will he find you waiting with your hand out to take what he has for you? That's not virtue, ladies, that's a beggar. As a daughter of the most high God we don't beg…we bring. We bring our own stuff to the table so when our king arrives he finds a queen.

Men, what will you have when you find her? A MAN who finds a wife finds a good thing. A man has his ducks all in a row and he is not looking for a woman to take care of him. A man fully understands his role as a husband and he is looking for his help mate. He is looking for the woman that owns the rib of his side; he is looking for his "better half". A man knows who he is long before he meets his bride. He is secure in himself as a man. He knows what he wants and already has much of it.

While you're waiting, child of God…work on YOU!

Kingdom Leaders and Worshippers
The Ambassadors

In order to be an effective leader you must be a heart and spirit-filled worshipper. It is through your worship that you discover "The Truth". Jesus Christ visits with you in this place to build a relationship with you and to give you instruction on how to live a life as a Kingdom Leader: An Ambassador!

Here we will share various forms of worship and leadership styles in order for you to find your place of dominion. All leaders has one thing in common, they have dominion over something. As Ambassadors we were created to have dominion over nature, the atmosphere and all the elements that reside in the earth. Jesus Christ illustrates the power we have access to when he commands the seas to become peaceful. He also demonstrates our power when he healed the sick and cast out demons and other unclean spirits. In these ways and many others, Christ demonstrates how we are to operate as Ambassadors for the Kingdom...Thy Kingdom Come, thy will be done on earth as it is in heaven... This should be done by us...His Ambassadors.

My Worship Is For Real

Worship is defined as a reverent love and devotion expressed in varies forms paying honor and homage. Our lives are designed to be a form of worship as we give honor to God daily. It is His desire and He seeks those that display both private and public worship performed in "spirit and in truth" *(John 4:24)*.

These are the elements of worship: praying, singing, reading, volunteering and preaching. These work individually as well as collectively.

Prayer

When we pray we make our requests to God with adoration, confession, supplication, or thanksgiving. As a worshipper and leader prayer is necessary in order to achieve all that God would have you to be. The bible says in Luke 18:1 "*...men ought always to pray and not to faint...*" Through prayer; especially as a leader, it gives you strength to endure the tasks that a human can not handle alone. Prayer is our open line of communication with God. You cannot have a relationship without communication and therefore you cannot have a relationship with God without prayer. Nothing and no one should have the power to disrupt your prayer life.

Jesus told them a story showing that it was necessary for them to pray consistently and never quit. (Luke 18:1 – The Message)

We find Daniel doing just this very thing even though the king decreed that no one pray or worship any other god except the king himself. Daniel, knowing what had been decreed kneeled and prayed to God nevertheless. (Daniel 6:10) As a leader it is important that you seek God first through prayer. *"But seek ye first the kingdom of God, and his righteousness; and all these things shall be added unto you." (Matthew 6:33 - KVJ)*

Jeremiah 33: 2-3 from the Message bible say it so plainly:

"This is God's Message, the God who made earth, made it livable and lasting, known everywhere as God: 'Call to me and I will answer you. I'll tell you marvelous and wondrous things that you could never figure out on your own."

"Ask and it will be given to you; seek and you will find; knock and the door will be opened to you. For everyone who asks receives; he who seeks finds; and to him who knocks, the door will be opened. (Matthew 7:7-8 – NKJV)

Your pray is the most important form of communication that you have with Him. It's the bridge between you and Him and each word you speak take you another closer to Him. Through your prayer you enter into the throne room. As Kingdom leader you must pray, pray, and then pray some more… God continually invites us and encourages us to ask Him for help because He wants to bless us.

Give all your worries and cares to God, for he cares about you. (1 Peter 5:7 – NLT)

Rule of thumb: God won't give directions to a person who isn't seeking direction from Him. Nor will anyone else seek directions from you if you haven't sought direction from Him. That's like having the blind leading the blind.

THY KINGDOM COME

Singing

"Praise the Lord! Sing to the Lord a new song. Sing his praises in the assembly of the faithful. (Psalm 149:1 – NLT)

Singing is an expression of how we feel about something or someone. It is the poetry crafted to instrumental notes that are created to flow and become an art form of its own. Singing is a pure expression from your heart.

Everyone has a song that reminds them of a memory in time. We sing the Happy Birthday song to our friends and family. We all somehow know all the words to Aretha Franklin's anthem, R.E.S.P.E.C.T. and every couple has "their song". God wants a song too. The Lord delights in the praises of His people and as a leader and worshipper it is important to find your own song so through the good times and the bad time you have something to uplift you or sustain you. Singing is just another way of communicating with God just to tell Him how much you love Him. It expresses what you feel or what you may be presently going through. Praising God in song is your best weapon against the enemy because when you praise God you are showing all powers, principalities, and demons of darkness that your great God is worthy of praise, regardless of your circumstance. Praise produces victory and victory evokes more praise. Even if you can't sing a note in tune, it still sounds like music to His ears because your praises are coming straight from your heart and your praise reaches His heart.

"Sing a new song to the Lord! Let the whole earth sing to the Lord! Sing to the Lord; praise his name. Each day proclaim the good news that he saves. (Psalm 96:1-2. – NLT)

Reading

In order to be an effective leader you must read and study the word of God and other materials that will assist you as you get closer to Him. Through reading you open your mind to Him so that He can show you a world beyond that in which we live. Studying the word of God is an open invitation into the spirit realm. It is in the Word of God we unlock the mysteries of life. God reveals more of himself to us as we study the word of God. It is through the word of God that He guides us into our destiny.

"Study to shew thyself approved unto God, a workman that needeth not to be ashamed, rightly dividing the word of truth." (2 Timothy 2:15 – KJV)

In whatever capacity you hold, whether it be a preacher, teacher, psalmist, wife, husband, parent, mentor, or counselor it is important to study your craft, surroundings, industry, and most importantly the Word of God so that you become more perfect in Him and an example to others. A great leader only needs to walk and others will surely follow.

Volunteering

"I beseech you therefore, brethren, by the mercies of God, that ye present your bodies a living sacrifice, holy, acceptable unto God, which is your reasonable service." (Romans 12:1 – KJV)

Giving your time is part of that "reasonable service" God looks for from every worshippers and leaders. A great leader is one who will get out there and do it even when no one is watching or following. It is through your example that causes others to follow. In doing this you show humility and your love for the One you serve. Jesus gives us this example as He washes the feet of his disciples. In order to lead others you must be willing to show others that you, just like them, are here to serve. We all have a gift that is designed to serve others.

Each one should use whatever gift he has received to serve others, faithfully administering God's grace in its various forms.
(1 Peters 4:10 – NIV)

Preaching

Luke 4:16-19 gives a clear picture of the role of the preacher and motivator:

When he came to the village of Nazareth, his boyhood home, he went as usual to the synagogue on the Sabbath and stood up to read the Scriptures. The scroll of Isaiah the prophet was handed to him. He unrolled the scroll and found the place where this was written: "The Spirit of the Lord is upon me, for he has anointed me to bring Good News to the poor. He has sent me to proclaim that captives will be released, that the blind will see, that the oppressed will be set free, and that the time of the Lord's favor has come."
(New Living Translation)

Preaching is an anointing that comes straight from heaven. You are given the gift to preach, teach, inspire, motivate, chastise, and convict. This scripture describes the purpose of a preacher's life. In this passage Jesus was in his hometown attending a church service. As he read the scripture he also declared his destiny to the church. When you are called to preach it is an anointing. Every preacher's anointing is different but the message is still the same. You are anointed to bring God's good news to all who will hear it. The anointed message God has placed inside you should set the captives free. It should open blinded eyes so that every man, woman, boy and girl can see that Jesus Christ is the way. Your message and your life should shine brightly declaring to the world the goodness of your Savior.

No one can teach you how to preach. Preachers are born, not raised. It is an anointing, a seed that God has to place on the inside of you. At some point in your life that seed will grow and your gift begins to shine. A preacher can preach in a parking lot. A preacher can invoke change in your life even when he/she isn't trying to. It's second nature. It becomes like breathing. You're always preaching, teaching, and empowering. It's who you are. You can be taught how to enhance the gift and how to use it more effectively, but no one can be taught how to preach.

"What do I preach?" That is the question many preachers, pastors, ministers, and teachers alike ask on a weekly basis.

Every message comes from God. It's His message after all. Why not seek Him in the process. Here's a prayer that we pray every week as we begin the process of preaching and teaching God's message:

"Lord as I begin preparing Your sermon
I ask that You would bless me and anoint me.
I ask for Your wisdom and Your grace.
Lord, please unfold the mysteries of the gospel to my heart and then anoint me to deliver that which I clearly understand to your people.
I ask that you would bless right now the people that will hear it and let their hearts begin now to receive that which they will hear on Sunday.
Let this sermon be life changing.
Let it be burden removing and yolk destroying.
In Jesus' name, amen"

There is a lot to be said on preaching; quite frankly enough to fill an entire library. The most important thing that should be said is always remember whose message you are preaching:
The good news has nothing to do with the preacher and everything to do with the Savior!

Find Your Leadership Style and Stick with It

In his grace, God has given us different gifts for doing certain things well. So if God has given you the ability to prophesy, speak out with as much faith as God has given you. If your gift is serving others, serve them well. If you are a teacher, teach well. If your gift is to encourage others, be encouraging. If it is giving, give generously. If God has given you leadership ability, take the responsibility seriously. And if you have a gift for showing kindness to others, do it gladly. (Romans 12:6-8 NLT)

Finally, you have found your place in the Kingdom! You are an Ambassador! You have authority and dominion. You are a natural born leader. Now what?

Now it's time to understand the direction of your leadership. Everyone is a leader. The clear definition of a leader is one who has the ability to influence others. Every Ambassador is a leader. You might be a pastor, minister, teacher, mother, father, business executive or student. You are a leader. As we sat down to write this book we began to reflect on our different leadership styles. We are ministers in the same great church, Word Kingdom Ministries; however, we all have different leadership styles. And you now what? It works. Actually it works well. We began to ponder our leadership styles and also the leadership styles of others who have influenced our lives. The gift of leadership is referenced in Romans chapter 12 but we must clearly understand that leaders are unique individuals. Below we have put together six different styles of leadership.

The Motivator

The motivating leader is the one who finds change exciting. The motivator is the one in the room cheering every time God moves. The motivator can fire up the crowd, celebrate your accomplishments, and offer correction in a way that makes you feel good about it. Jesus is the prime example as he motivated the disciples to leave everything they knew, including booming businesses, to follow him. He inspired them in ways they clearly understood. He knew when to work and when to rest. He knew when to fast and when to feast. He even changed a few names!

A motivating leader is always thinking of ways to inspire his people to get the job done. They clearly understand that sometimes disciples get discouraged or lose focus. Here's where a motivator shines. A motivator won't get angry with the disciples, instead a motivator will seize this as an opportunity to inspire and empower the disciples.

Jesus gives a perfect example for a motivator when several disciples had been fishing all night to no avail. It was Jesus who motivated professional fisherman to try it once more. He motivated them to give it one last try and when they did they reaped a harvest so big they needed others to help haul it all in. That's motivational leadership at its best!

The Directional/Strategic Leader

Directional and Strategic leaders have the ability to take a vision and lead others in a direct path. These leaders do what motivators often can't do. A directional/strategic leader puts the vision into motion. They compel others to action. A directional/strategic leader always has a game plan. This plan is one everyone can understand and work with. A directional/strategic leader is able to manage several ministries or teams simultaneously without losing the big picture. The directional/strategic leader is the person who is able to manage the vision and make sure everything gets done decently and in order.

The Team/Bridge-Building Leader

The Team/Bridge leader is the one who encourages other to be a part of the team (the church). The Team/Bridge leader acts like a trainer. When we play as a team, we accomplish the God-given vision for His church. The Team leader knows how to build an effective team and this leader knows how to get all the Ambassadors to work together. Jesus is the Coach. He's given us the play book, and he's calling the plays. It's up to the Ambassadors to run the plays, and when we do, everyone wins. Paul stated it so well when he said it, *Let there be real harmony so there won't be divisions in the church. I plead with you to be of one mind, united in thought and purpose. (1 Corinthians 1:10 – NLT)*

A team/bridge building leader knows if you place the right people in the right positions only then can you produce the best results.

T-- together / E--each / A--accomplishes / M—more

The Visionary / Entrepreneur

Visionary and entrepreneurial leaders are one in the same for this very reason: they both envision hope and possibilities. Every leader receives a vision from God; however, a visionary leader will do everything possible to make that vision a reality. A visionary leader is not easily discouraged. In fact, the more impossible the situation, the more they go after it. Visionary leaders don't care what other say, they only know what they saw and that vision will surface by any means necessary. As a visionary and entrepreneur you accept the challenge of standing in between the spiritual realm and natural realms operating as conduit causing a higher level of thought and tangible grasp of reality. You open the eyes of those that can't quite see or those that are completely blind and you show them the realm of possibilities through God. You are the one who draws people into the vision and once they see it, they'll follow you anywhere.

The Shepherding Leader

The Shepherd understands that empowering God's people is all about helping, sharing, and ministering the word of God to the world – regardless if it's one or thousands. The Shepherd loves and nurtures his followers and supports them at all cost. The shepherding leader knows that his or her sole purpose in ministry is centered on respecting, encouraging, caring, loving and have a passion for the people of God. A Shepherd will not exploit or dictate to the people God has made him/her oversee of. The shepherd cultivates and brings out the gifts and talents of each individual and he/she does it with love and understanding. A shepherding leader doesn't see flaws or mistake, this leader only sees the heart of the person. As a Kingdom Shepherd remember to guard your thoughts; they become you words. Consider your words; they become your actions. Examine your actions; they become your habits. Watch your habits; they become your character. Demonstrate your character; it becomes your destiny. Embrace your destiny, it confirms you.

The Managing Leader

As an orchestra conductor ensures each section come in precisely at the right time, a managing leader ensures that all components are working melodiously together so that all thing work together. One that manages well knows that management does not mean dictatorship but partnership and a managing leader is your partner. The task of managing can be tedious and overwhelming to other leaders but not for the managing leader. The managing leader is anointed to manager. Just as Christ walked this earth He gathered twelve disciples to support His earthly ministry and managed them even to the point they didn't even know that they were being managed. Can you imagine feeding five thousand men (and more) on a hot summer day and working with a team instructing them on how to distribute the food, making sure that everyone was fed? That's great management!

It was His passion for the mission and His excellent managerial skills that cause His disciples to become involved and stay involved in the ministry even after His crucifixion and resurrection. Jesus was such a great manager, even after he left the earth in the physical realm his disciples were still able to carry on the mission.

Final Thoughts

When all is said and done, you are an Ambassador. Your purpose is to ensure God's will be done in earth as it is in heaven. Your success as an Ambassador is not based on what you accomplish. It is not based on how much you acquire. Your success will be measured based on what you leave behind. When you leave this earth, just like Jesus, your mission should continue. It will continue in those you have influenced, those you have led. You are a "Good News" Ambassador. It's time to get to work tell any and everyone about your Lord and Savior, Jesus Christ.

Now all glory to God, who is able to keep you from falling away and will bring you with great joy into his glorious presence without a single fault. All glory to him who alone is God, our Savior through Jesus Christ our Lord. All glory, majesty, power, and authority are his before all time, and in the present, and beyond all time! Amen. (Jude 1:24-25 – NLT)

God bless you!

About The Authors

Ambassador Andrea D. Wilson

Andrea is an anointed woman of God who has enriched so many lives with her dynamic speaking engagements and empowerment counseling services. Andrea began her journey as a motivational speaker and counselor recognizing her passion to help people live the abundant life Christ came to give.

On March 19, 2000, Andrea became the first woman ever licensed as a minister in the over 50 year old traditional Baptist church, New St. John Community MB Church in Chicago , Illinois . On November 24, 2002, Andrea was installed as the Pastor of Word Kingdom Ministries in Chicago , Illinois .

In March 2007 Andrea founded Fullness of Life an empowerment program for women, teens and youth designed to offer the necessary tools for living a successful, prosperous life.

Andrea lives in a Chicago suburb, with her husband and daughter. She is currently working on her first fiction novel.

Ambassador Tamora R. Walls

Tamora has a heart for ministry; she is ready and willing to give the best to God and to His people. Tamora was called to the ministry to preach the gospel in 2000 where she began to operate in the anointing as the leader of the Women's Ministry and an Intercessor of Prayer at Greater New Mt. Eagle MB Church. Over the years, she has been invited to speak at different events for various churches in Illinois. As of November, 2005 she joined Word Kingdom Ministries in Chicago, where her pastor is Minister Andrea Wilson. On November, 2006 she was licensed as a Minster of the Gospel. She is currently the Minister of Music for the Word Kingdom Praise Team, Power of the Word Bible teacher and part of the evangelistic empowerment team.

Ambassador Walls began a business partnership with Business Services Group as an independent contractor which offers business solutions to profit, non-profit, and small business institutions. She also offers technical skills and services which include graphic design, presentations, computer training, IT support, web developing, business planning and grant writing. Tamora graduated from Columbia College of Chicago and just finished writing a fiction novel entitled "Reflections of the Heart".

Ambassador Eunice Wade

Eunice possess the gift to see the inner beauty of the battered, tattered, dismantled, and what others would abandon and label as trash. With God's Wisdom she sees beyond what the world perceive and only catch a glimpse of, and draws out the essence of God in each individual so that they and the world can see it too. Ambassador Wade was licensed as Minister of the Gospel in 2004 at Greater King David M.B. Church.

Through her gift to give of herself she was called by God to start a non-profit organization called, "Talitha Cumi Ministries" by which hundreds of young girls (starting at the age 12) and women have been blessed by powerful workshops, weekend spa retreats, training skills classes, youth outreach retreats, holiday and shelter donation events and more.

Minister Wade joined the Word Kingdom family in December of 2006 and her presence and gifts have aided the ministry to move to the next level in God. Her passion in the near future is to open a housing community for women and their children who have challenges and need the support to "ARISE" and from her heart she speaks to all God's daughters "Little Girl, Get Up"!